To: Boya —
May this book
empower & Inspire you
to Reach for
all your's

JOHNNETTA MCSWAIN

RISING

ABOVE THE

SCARS

"Failure Is Not An Option"

Dream Wright Publications, LLC
Atlanta, GA

Dream Wright Publications, LLC

P.O. Box 1914
Powder Springs, GA 30127

Second Edition: March 2011
Revised: September 2011

First printing: November 2010 by Dream Wright Publications.

Some names and identifying details have been changed to protect the privacy of individuals.

ISBN 978-0-615-45301-9

Cover Design by Marion Designs
Book Design by Lady Dragonfly Publishing

Printed in the United States of America.

10 9 8 7 6 5 4 3 2

DEDICATION

This book is dedicated to my momma and sister for being brave enough to join forces with me and share parts of their painful life stories in order to help empower women worldwide.

And to my sons, RaShod and Jahleel, who were never ashamed of me and the life I once lived—and who loved me regardless of what I couldn't give them. I dedicate this book to you both.

RaShod, you never gave me any problems while growing up. You have blossomed into a strong and handsome young man. Any momma would be proud.

Jahleel, you are super smart and handsome, too. Please don't worry about whether there will be any cycles left for you to break. You will have plenty of cycles to break in your own family.

I want to thank my husband, Willie, for supporting me in his own special way. Thank you for allowing me to chase my vision. And thank you for understanding why I have to tell my story. Thank you for marrying me when you knew my past wasn't that of the Virgin Mary.

ACKNOWLEDGEMENTS

Jane Fonda, Pamela Roberts and Debbie Day; Georgia Public Broadcasting (GPB); Thyra and Richard Zeits; Renew Design Studios; Marion Designs; Lady Dragonfly Publishing & Design; Erin Howarth; Akbar and Daphne Cujoe; Kennesaw Sate University (KSU) Department of Communication; KSU Office of Development; KSU Siegel Institute For Leadership, Ethics & Character; SafePath Children's Advocacy Center, Inc.; Peach County Family Connection; Party with A Purpose, Inc.; Fort Valley State University (FVSU); Clark Atlanta University (CAU) TV; Forsyth County Domestic Violence Task Force; DeKalb County Schools; Atlanta Journal Constitution (AJC); Families First; and the Unity Fellowship Church.

I would also, like to thank The Alliance of Southwest Missouri; Economic Security Corporation; National Association of Social Workers (NASW); Trenay Perry Bynum; Pine-Sol; End Violence Against Women (EVAW); Campbell Publicity LLC; Atlanta Regional Council for Higher Education; Human Services Department Office of Aging; Atlanta Press Club; Georgia Department of Human Resources; Live Your Legacy, with Aurea McGarry; Prevent Child Abuse Georgia; South Cobb High School; Schusters Cash, LLC; Georgia Writers Association; Dr. Betty L. Siegel; Kidz2leaders, Inc.; Dr. Lauri Grossman; Dr. Linda Stillman; Onslow County Department of Social Services; and The Leader Tribune.

SPECIAL THANKS

I want to first give thanks to my almighty God for choosing me at birth to be a vessel to deliver this powerful message of hope, forgiveness, faith, love, resiliency, and the belief that anything is possible if you dream. I want to thank God for never letting me go my own way when I was in those dangerous streets, acting like a fool.

I want to thank my brother-in-law, Derrick for supporting me in every way. Thank you for baby sitting, house sitting, taking me to the airport, and much more. You are a great brother-in-law. I love you. I want to thank a special mentor and friend, Marlon Campbell; we were truly destined to cross paths and work together. Thank you for believing in me and my story.

I want to thank my Breaking the Cycle, Beating the Odds, team members, Sonja Motes, Lisa Levin, Alice Hutchinson, and Natascha Sherrod, for all of your dedication and hard work. I want to thank my jeweler Darlene Bedford, Allie Rose Jewelry Designs, for her vision, creation and designing Breaking the Cycle, Beating the Odds, Hope bracelets and my signature set I wear to all of my speaking engagements. I want to thank my mentees, Tomeka and Keba for hanging in there with me.

I can't leave out my best friends, Tammi, Shellina, Karen, Marlisa and Valencia, for putting up with me for over 20 years. I also, want to thank each of you for allowing me to share some of the many obstacles we faced in our friendship. I hope this book will help other women realize the importance of having girlfriends. It is truly a gift. I wouldn't trade anything for the love, laughter, heartaches, tears, disappointments, good times and the sistahood.

My church friends, Cassandra, Tweety, Pamela C., Pamela (Mookey), Andrea, Sharon, Lanita, Nilaja and Paula, thank you for the 30 years of friendship. This is where it all started. We have been through a lot together growing up in the church. We had to stay strong for each other. Thank you for treating me like family, even though I left the church a long time ago. To my special friends, Stephaney Vaughn, Wanda, Tywanna and Tomika, thank you for all the good times we had in the streets and all the love you all showed me. To my little sisters, Dee and Von, we have been together since you were teenagers and now you're grown women with children. I love you till the end of time.

I want to thank Dr. Susan Kossak of Clark Atlanta University (CAU), Whitney M. Young of the School of Social Work, who are my mentor, supporter, friend, colleague, sista, and girl friend. Thank you for writing your book, "Reaching In, Reaching Out" sharing our amazing relational journey for the world to realize mentors has no origin, race, social status, class, culture, sex, or gender. I adore you.

To my college friends, Julia, Stephaney, Jennene, Kiko, Christy, and Nikao, thank you all for meeting me at the student center every-day, eight years ago and listening to me talk about my dream. Although most of you have relocated, you still take out time to fly to Atlanta and support my many projects. Thank you for purchasing raffle tickets, and sending money to make sure I get to my workshops and confer-ences going. Thank you. I love you.

I want to thank Chaun Archer with Lady Dragonfly Publishing & Design who believed in my story, pushed me and encouraged me to write this book. We started this book journey together and I am grateful for all of your hours of dedication, help and assistance with this project.

I want to thank my first editor Erin Howarth, who from the very first time we spoke on the phone, took this project, and made sure my voice and message was captured throughout. I want to thank my second editors, Akbar and Daphne Cujoe. Thank you for having compassion, empathy, love, patience and understanding the urgency of why I needed to write this book. Thank you for the many long hours you put in to make this book successful. Thank you for believing in me and understanding my mission to break the silence of abuse. Thanks for allowing me to keep it real. I have a new found respect for editors. I can't wait for us to write my next book. You are truly the best editors in the world. I will always love you.

To all the people I might have left out, by mistake and/or on purpose. Thank you for playing a valuable part in my life; whether you were a hater or a motivator; whether it was for a day, a month, a year or a season.

CONTENTS

CONTENTS

"Making your mark on the world is hard. If it were easy, everybody would do it. But it's not. It takes patience, it takes commitment, and it comes with plenty of failure along the way. The real test is not whether you avoid this failure, because you won't. It's whether you let it harden or shame you into inaction, or whether you learn from it; whether you choose to persevere."

—Barack Obama

INTRODUCTION

Escape is not something that can always be accomplished physically, sometimes we need to have an outlet. Some people drink, use drugs, and have sex, while others write or even exercise. As a small, fragile, five-year-old growing up in Birmingham, Alabama—I didn't have many choices.

I remember dreaming I was Wonder Woman; my sister, Sonya, believed she was Superwoman; and my cousin, James, was Superman. Together, we were the Super Friends. As the Super Friends, we were going to eliminate the monsters that were physically and sexually abusing us. This was so real to us that we made costumes of each superhero and role played in our grandmomma's backyard.

We imagined how we would destroy the monsters and get rid of the fear of living to endure another day of brutal abuse. The jingle of Grandmomma's keys and the click of her heels against the hardwood floor, as she prepared to leave for church, were all it took to bring us back to our harsh reality. Once her car engine started, I could feel my legs start to quiver and my body grow weak. It gave us the surest indication of what was coming next.

PART 1

FORGOTTEN INNOCENCE

FAMILY

I was born to Jeanette Tate and Nathaniel McSwain, on January 31, 1970. My only sister, Sonya Tate, was born 11 months earlier. My father was not a part of our lives. At a young age, I can remember feeling that we were an inconvenience, even to my momma. She was adamant about her feelings toward motherhood. Simply put, she did not want to be a mother.

My momma and her sisters were all sexually abused by my granddaddy, and as in most households where abuse takes place, it simply wasn't talked about. It was as if folks believed that remaining quiet would somehow make it all go away. In reality, it didn't go away; it only helped the ones who failed to protect the abused to avoid their feelings of guilt.

As soon as Momma turned 16, she dropped out of high school and began running the streets with her two girlfriends. They all had special nicknames. Momma was called, "Do It If You Want To." Her friends were "Do It If You Can" and "Do It When You Can."

Momma drank heavily, partied feverishly, and fought hard.

She believed in fighting. I believe she decided that she had not fought hard enough as a child, so she would never again miss another opportunity to do so.

In 1972, we left Alabama and Momma was running for her life. She and her baby sister had gone out one night with a well-respected male friend from the neighborhood. They knew he was married, and even knew his wife, so they intended to have a few drinks and just hang out.

He took them to a local hangout spot near the airport. This was where everybody hooked up back in the day. They had a good time drinking, talking about life, reminiscing about the past, and enjoying themselves as planned.

On this particular night, they were the only ones at the typically crowded hangout spot. All of a sudden, the mood changed and Momma had a gut feeling that something was wrong. She noticed the way he began to look at her sister. The man they thought of as a friend was becoming too "friendly." Momma and her sister began hinting their disinterest in anything sexual and that they were ready to leave.

Momma could see a demon rise within him and take control. Enraged, he picked up a pipe and struck her sister across the face with a powerful blow, fracturing her jaw in two places. Since they did not want to "give it up," he said they would not leave there alive; however, he was unaware that Momma didn't go anywhere without being strapped. She usually carried small hatchets or machetes; she was always armed with something.

Propelled by her sister's motionless body lying in a heap on the ground, when he came at Momma, she grabbed the lead pipe he held and then deftly swung around him with her knife primed. Her mind snapped, as flashes of him hurting her sister fueled her adrenaline.

With fury, Momma plunged the blade of the knife into every

vulnerable part of his body within reach; primarily, the neck and shoulder. Blood was everywhere.

Fortunately for him and Momma he made it to the hospital alive and survived the attack. As for my aunt, her mouth had to be wired shut.

After being released from the hospital, he would continuously call my grandmomma's house hoping to reach Momma. Each time he called, he would tell her, "It ain't over, bitch. Yo ass is mine! You betta' not let me catch you. I'mma fuck you up!"

Finally, one of his calls had a distinctly different tone. Momma instinctively knew that he was genuine that time. Later that day, she called her brother in Detroit and asked him if she could move in with her two children. The next day, we moved to Detroit. After a few years there, Momma grew bored and tired. She longed for home and the feeling of something familiar.

One day, after Momma had an argument with my uncle, we left his house and started walking back to Alabama from Detroit. To this day, I cannot remember how we really got back to Alabama, but I know we didn't walk.

Soon after returning to Birmingham, Momma picked right up where she left off running the streets. We moved back in with Grandmomma and Momma stopped coming around. She only returned occasionally to bathe and get a change of clothes. Because she knew Grandmomma disapproved of her fast lifestyle, she hated it at there and rarely visited.

Momma's life was very unstable. Although she had faced abuse from our granddaddy in that house, I believe she felt we were safe. Besides, Momma didn't have enough to offer Sonya and me. She felt having a roof over our heads and a sure meal was better than her two little girls running the streets with her.

The front of Grandmomma's house was covered with red brick and gray siding and seemed large to a child; not because of the structure, but how it miraculously fit so many people. At times, we had 10 people living under that roof all at once; however, it was quite small. There were three small bedrooms, a living room, one bathroom, a kitchen, and a back room. My grandparents, great-uncle, three uncles, two aunts, three cousins, sister and I all lived there. Sometimes, when there weren't enough places to sleep, we had to sleep on the old, hard, wooden floor, which had splinters and nails sticking out of it.

Despite the house being overcrowded, Grandmomma still found room for her stuff. She was a pack rat and found it hard to throw anything away. She kept everything in bags around the house. The place was so infested with roaches that I had grown to think of it as normal. There were a few rats in there, too; however, she always kept cats in and around the house to keep their population low.

Eventually, Grandmomma extended the house by having a small room built onto the living room. She also added new siding in place of the wood that the termites had devoured. She called this room, "The New Room." This room was intended for company only. She bought new furniture and a brand-new organ to outfit this addition. The room was treated like the Oval Office in the White House.

There is something sacred about new things to those who do not come by new things easily. Whatever is new, or even gently used, takes on an air of extreme importance and priority. It is cherished and overvalued. Along with everyone else, I truly believed "The New Room" was something of remarkable value and held it in high esteem. We worked very hard to make sure it appeared new for as long as possible.

My uncles and aunts would talk about me, Sonya, and our cousins, as if we were invisible; as if we were nothing. They talked about how irresponsible our mommas were for leaving us there for months at a time without ever calling to see how we were doing. They would buy tempting foods, dangle it in front of us like we were dogs, and then dare us to ask for some. I could feel my mouth salivate and my stomach churn craving just the slightest taste.

They showed favoritism toward some of the children and played us against each other to make us feel inferior. We were almost being treated like slaves on plantations. Some of us were beaten and blamed more than others; beaten for silly and petty things to show us they were bigger and stronger, and to instill fear in our youthful hearts. We were not allowed to go anywhere with them or ask for anything. We were constantly told we were ugly, and reminded that our mommas did not want us, and that we should be grateful they put up with us.

My grandparents were not like the ones that appeared on television. They did not spoil and shower us with love and affection. Furthermore, they did not even sleep in the same bed. They had hard lives and it showed.

My granddaddy was a big man. He was the man of the house and as mean as a snake. Granddaddy had diabetes, which he referred to as having "sugar," and had surgery on his feet because of it. Grandmomma constantly warned us not to step on his feet. We were so aware of this that we were exceptionally careful around him. It became second nature to glide around his feet as we got near him. If we happened to bump into his foot by accident, I think it hurt us more than it did him because we felt so guilty that maybe he would have to have them cut off completely. Regardless of Granddaddy's condition, it did not stop him from getting around and working hard without complaint. I have never seen a man who worked as hard as Granddaddy. He made sure he brought food in the house, cooked, paid the bills, and cleaned the house. He gave Grandmomma everything she needed and even found time to sing in the church choir on Sunday.

He had what we called a "gem belt," which was a long piece of broken, worn-out rubber used as a fan belt on most cars. He would beat us with it. Sometimes in the early winter morning hours, he would use his gem belt to rouse us out of a warm, sound sleep to go outside in the cold, dark backyard to gather pre-cut wood and medium-sized pieces of black coal for the furnace. This furnace sat in the middle of the living room floor where we slept. We all had to fill up the tin foot tubs and the large, thick, white plastic buckets and take them back into the house to feed the furnace.

Our duties were many. On Saturday mornings, we had to get up before sunrise, long before the cartoons that ran on television to help wash and hang clothes on the clothesline Granddaddy had made from some kind of rope or fishing line. We didn't complain, but I would be lying if I said that we didn't think of the cartoons every second. The thought of seeing them gave us energy to complete the jobs quickly, hoping that we would catch at least one.

The clothes were washed by hand on a large rub board until Grandmomma finally got a washing machine. It happened to be the kind that only washed clothes. We still had to rinse them in a large, galvanized foot tub and wring them out as dry as we could. Then, we had to run them through the roller press placed on top of the washing machine to drain the excess water before hanging them out to dry. We were not exempt from cutting the grass, either. On top of that, we were expected to kill the chickens and pluck their feathers to prepare them for dinner. We knew we had to do it.

"Cause television was for adults," if the adults didn't have company over, and we finished in time, we were allowed to watch the rest of the cartoons on the single black and white television that sat in the corner of the living room. Since, "children had no place on Grandmomma's nice furniture," we had to sit on the nasty, cold hardwood floors.

We called my grandmomma Madea; a name commonly used in the south, which generally referred to grandmothers. It is a shortened version of momma dear. Grandmomma was light. She was a caramel-colored, short, chubby, no-nonsense, mean old woman. She spent most of her life as a housewife raising eight children: three girls and five boys.

For years, Grandmomma was very sick due to kidney failure. She went to dialysis at least twice each week and would complain about her health. Sometimes, she would even cry because she was in so much pain. I went with her to dialysis occasionally, but Sonya went almost every time. Grandmomma was meaner to me than she was to Sonya. She would pick my sister up and hold her in her arms, singing to her while rocking in her rocking chair. She made it clear that Sonya was her favorite.

Grandmomma was very impatient with people and cussed at anybody, anywhere including church but she wasn't always bad-tempered. She loved to fish and found solace doing so. She would take us on fishing trips, which I enjoyed. Every single thing we did, even leading up to the fishing trip, was exciting. We children found delight in the simple things and were not picky when there weren't many options.

We dug up the earthworms in the backyard to use as bait and made an adventure out of it. We would pack big lunches of bologna sandwiches and watermelon. Once we arrived at our destination, we ran around and played in the trees just letting our imaginations run wild.

Grandmomma's favorite was catfish. Sometimes, she would even let us try to catch some, but we were never very good at it; not as good as her, anyway. When we got back home from fishing, we would take the fish to the backyard to be skinned. We'd nail the catfish to a big tree in the backyard and make a slit behind its neck. Then, we'd use a pair of pliers to strip it of its skin.

Grandmomma would put a whole bucket of white lard in a big, black, steel pot heated by charcoal. Then, after seasoning and battering the fish in cornmeal, she would drop it in that hot lard until it floated to the top; golden brown and crispy. That was a sight we couldn't wait to see. We could eat as much as we wanted. There was always plenty of food. Despite all the work involved in taking a fish from the water to the dinner table, Grandmomma was more soft, delicate, relaxed, and peaceful during this time. And I enjoyed being around her then. Because of her increasing need for dialysis, our fishing trips became less frequent. It was sad, but the ones we did take were still memorable.

Grandmomma took on many roles, so many roles that the pressure started to take its toll on her. She took custody of my aunt's three children who were left on the front porch. She was also raising Sonya and me, not knowing if our momma would ever return.

Grandmomma could cook anything. On good days, we woke up to the smell of homemade biscuits, bacon, bologna, grits, and sausage. She had a garden filled with every vegetable imaginable. We rarely made trips to the grocery store for fruits or vegetables. She made us shuck corn and snap green beans. We also picked tomatoes, collard greens, cabbage, figs, and yellow and red watermelons. We would put everything in bags and Mason jars to freeze or preserve.

We raised live hogs, goats, and chickens in Grandmomma's backyard. When it was time to slaughter the animals, we all had to do our part. I can remember never going without something to eat. We did not eat at any fast food places or go out to restaurants. It wasn't necessary. On holidays, Grandmomma would make vanilla ice cream with an ice cream machine we had to turn by hand. She would make potato salad, macaroni and cheese, turnip and mustard greens, red velvet cake and butter pound cakes. She also made hot water corn bread in that big, black, steel skillet she had. Grandmomma would light up a huge grill in the backyard that Granddaddy made from a black barrel, and she'd barbecue ribs, chicken, and pork. We had the best time ever, running around playing Hide-n-Seek, One-Two-Three-Red-Light, Grandma Grey, and other childhood games.

When my momma did come around, it was always very brief. She looked so disconnected and unhappy. She did not ask how we were doing and didn't act like she missed us. There were no hugs and kisses. She didn't tell us that she loved us and she didn't bring us anything. We got so used to that treatment that we stopped getting our hopes up that she would take us with her. I think her visits were more for her own peace of mind, to see if we were still alive or if there was anything visibly wrong with us. I always could see it was painful for her to come home. She knew how my aunties and uncles, and even my grandparents, felt. She knew what they thought of her and they didn't hold their tongues on the subject. They looked at her with disgust and sometimes pity. It hurt. I could see it in her eyes. I'm not sure if it was because of her past or because she felt badly for not being there for us. Whatever the case may be, I believe she knew we were being mistreated but did not want to hear the words come from our mouths.

Beaten and Broken

By the time I was five years old, I had already started to believe that I was not only inferior, but I was also a child abandoned by her own momma. As a child, I had no place, no voice, and no worth at all. I was beaten so much that I was afraid to even make eye contact with an adult for fear of not showing that I was humble and grateful.

In elementary school, I was called "Scar Face," because my body was covered with scars, scratches, and burns—many of which remain today. We were beaten with switches, extension cords, shoes, gem belts, and whatever else the adults we lived with got their hands on. My aunties and uncles would beat us for anything we did. It felt like just waking up was sufficient. My momma wasn't any better. They all made us go down the big hill at my grandmomma's house and pick switches to bring back for them to whip us. If the switches were too little or weak, they would thrash us with them and then make us go back down the hill to get more.

I was beaten most for urinating in the bed, which I did every single night. My granddaddy would pull the covers off us to check our clothes to see if we were wet. Upon finding us soiled, he would wake us up with a gem belt—lashing on our legs, backs, and entire body. Sometimes, my aunties and uncles would punish us by dragging us out of bed and stripping us of our wet clothes.

Anyone who has ever urinated in the bed knows—no matter how hard you tried or what you told yourself, there was a certain time during sleep when you thought you were on the commode. The moment you let your guard down and allowed yourself to fully surrender to sleep, it would happen. Each time it happened to me, I would promise myself that it would be the last. I was so upset with myself, and could not understand why it occurred every night—even after I swore that it wouldn't.

There is one particular instance I remember more than the others. One night, my cousin, James, and I were asleep in the dead of winter. I was comfortable and warm and had drifted into a deep sleep. Once again, my own body betrayed me. The relief came as it always did; however, once the warm urine began to soak up the sheets, physical relief gave way to psychological terror. I prayed that Granddaddy would not check us that morning. James felt the warm urine on his side of the bed and woke up wondering if it was his mistake. I'm sure it was both of us. Our childlike exhaustion soon overcame our fear and we drifted back to sleep. The repeated snap of Granddaddy's gem belt across our wet and pissy asses soon awakened us. In order for us to learn our lesson, we were forced out onto the porch—undressed and entirely exposed to the elements. As we huddled together, I remember feeling so cold, I believed we would literally freeze to death. After several attempts to teach me my "lesson," in this cruel and unusual method, I eventually got really sick and was taken to the hospital. I had an extreme case of pneumonia, which had spread to my bones. As a result, I was hospitalized for almost a month. I don't remember anyone apologizing to me or feeling any semblance of compassion for what was done.

THE DIRTY LITTLE SECRET

My momma disappeared for weeks at a time, leaving us at my grandmomma's house. This was when the sexual abuse started at the hands of my three uncles, and occasionally my great-uncle. Sonya, James, and I were all around the ages of five and six.

My grandmomma loved going to church. Anytime the doors were open, she made sure to be there. Our uncles saw this as an opportunity to take advantage of the situation. As Grandmomma dressed and sang her hymns—preparing her spirit for a glorious time at church, my uncles were preparing for the worst. They would whisper to us about what they were planning to do once my grandmomma left.

I still remember the sick feeling in my stomach—as she prepared to leave. There were certain sounds that signaled to us her departure was nearing. With each one, my body would shut down a little more. The smell of her perfume made me grow weak. The jingle of her keys made my mouth go dry. The click-clack of her heels on the wooden floor made me shake. And, finally, the front door closing would prepare my body for what was about to happen.

My uncles were young; probably in their late teens and early twenties. One weighed over two hundred pounds and the other two were of average build. They would chase us down and drag us by our legs and feet from under the bed where we had run to hide. They tore our clothes off and then tied us up with ropes. We were naked and tied to chairs in the living room where they would sexually violate us for hours at a time; taking turns mounting us like musical chairs. We were forced to watch each other get assaulted. I dreaded every moment, knowing when it was my turn to watch and when it was my turn to be mounted.

We were just children experiencing and witnessing this horrific exploitation of our bodies, our minds, and our spirits. It was especially horrifying to watch my cousin, James, a young boy, being penetrated. James would be made to sit in the lap of either one of my uncles while being anally penetrated. He would scream out in anguish as his pride and boyhood were stolen. He fought, but like the rest of us, he was choked or beaten for fighting back. I cringed each time I heard his cries, but was powerless to help him. I would just close my eyes or look away as they laughed and smiled at each other—relishing the game they played with us. They were shameless and evident in regard to the great pleasure they shared by way of our unspeakable pain.

Sadistically, they would then order us to perform oral sex acts that made us gag and left our mouths sore. Afterward, they would ejaculate on our bodies and in our mouths, telling us semen was good for us and that it was okay to swallow because it tasted like creamed corn.

Sometimes, they would light up marijuana joints and make us smoke with them. They also bought pornographic magazines and made us flip through the pages to find centerfolds of naked women performing sexual acts on themselves. Once we found the photos, we would have to imitate these adult women, while they watched and masturbated. I felt so dirty—mirroring these sleazy images.

There were times when my sister and I slept together, because they would take turns coming into our bedroom to molest us. Sonya always fought back—no matter how they beat her. Many times, she would beg for them to take her instead of me. I can remember her screaming and crying profusely after being punched in the face and having her head beaten into the wall because she fought back. I simply lied there in fear for my life. Still, I was punched, choked, and threatened just the same.

Often, I was trapped beneath a man who weighed over two hundred pounds. I fought to breathe, praying that my asthma would not kick in or maybe hoping that it would. I would lay my body completely still, as the bed shook and squeaked. I could not feel the pain of his violation deeply rooted in my insides. I was forced to develop the ability to remove my spirit from this place and my mind from this scene of horror. I would become invisible. That was my newfound "superpower," and I used it well. It was used to the point where I did not cry or make a sound.

I felt sorry for my sister because I knew she had *no* power against them. I knew they were slowly destroying her mind. *If only she would let go*, I thought. I could feel myself trying to relay this message to her telepathically: *Let go, Sonya… just let go. Give them your body, but nothing else!*

She fought hard; not only for herself, but for me, too. They matched every effort of her childhood strength with manly blows that should have killed her. I don't know the precise moment it happened, but I lost my sister back then. A part of her died in that house.

My uncles were the monsters we wanted to destroy. They treated us like we were trash that was ready to be thrown away. We were not treated like children. For that matter, we were not treated like we shared the same blood as them pumping through our veins. The horror of being penetrated by such large men went far beyond the physical pain. It obliterated any sense of peace I might have had because it destroyed my faith in all adults. Feeling my uncles' large, masculine hands around my small neck—squeezing it every time I wiggled or turned to see if Sonya and James were all right, did more than cut off my air; it crushed my spirit.

One after the other, as they climbed on top of me, I became more and more numb to the thumping pain I felt. At night, alone in the bathroom, I would attempt to wash my blood-soaked panties out in the sink so no one would know what was happening. The next morning when I had to wash up for school, the thumping continued in my raw, sore vagina. Many days, I walked to school gap-legged because my legs would be so sore and bruised from being forced open for hours.

On occasion, my great-uncle, who was wheelchair-bound, would make me go in the back room, where he would take out his penis and force me to sit in his lap while he penetrated me. He made me sit there until he ejaculated. There was no safe place or safe person in my grandmomma's house.

They threatened to kill us if we told anyone. They had never given us a reason to doubt that they would not make good on their threats. Anyone who could do what they did to us surely had the potential to kill us. The reasons behind the inhumane torture we were made to suffer at their hands were never made clear to us. Perhaps such brutality never has a reason, it just is. The repercussions of that brutality were far-reaching and surpassed anything our young minds could grasp. We were robbed of our innocence by the very people who were supposed to protect us. We were made to feel worthless and powerless by the very people who were supposed to infuse us with a sense of self-worth. We were made to doubt the things we instinctively knew were right by the very people who were supposed to teach us right from wrong. It all remained our dirty little secret for the next five to six years.

NOWHERE TO RUN

One day after starting kindergarten, I was playing out in the backyard and stepped on a nail that pierced my foot. After I cried for dear life, Grandmomma pulled the nail out, wrapped my foot with a piece of raw fatback, and tied it up with a piece of white cloth made from an old bed sheet. We didn't go to the hospital, unless we had stopped breathing. Grandmomma had a remedy for everything.

We had to walk to school every morning down a steep hill and through a shortcut. On our journey, there was a rusty fence with a small hole cut out—just big enough for our little bodies to squeeze through. The day after my accident with the nail, Sonya, James, and I were walking home from school when an older boy started running after us. We did not know why he was chasing us down, but our natural instincts told us to run fast. We began to run—and in no time—Sonya and James had crawled through the hole in the fence. I could not make it through the fence as quickly as they did, because my foot was wrapped up and throbbing in answer to each of my frantic steps.

I stood trembling in fear and uncertainty. I looked ahead in the direction in which my sister and cousin had run, hoping they would realize I was missing and decide to come back for me. I then looked back in the direction of my chaser—praying that this boy didn't want to hurt me. I caught sight of him approaching, and the rest of my prayer quivered and died in my throat, settling down into the pit of my stomach. He led me to the other side of the fence—where we could not be easily seen—as I gave a last hopeful glance toward the hole in the fence. He asked if I would mind him doing *it* to me, as he started pulling down my panties. I said, "No. I don't mind." I didn't know what else to say. I was alone and my welfare rested in his hands.

Sex had long since become a tool for my survival. So much so, that it almost didn't seem strange or unusual that this latest transgression against my body was happening. There was little that this boy could take from me that had not already been taken by my uncles. My innocence had been totally and forever removed, before he ever met me at the fence. I cried the whole time he was assaulting me. I stared into the distance, expecting Sonya to come and rescue me, but no one ever came. I felt abandoned. I just stood there, wondering why he was doing this to me. When he was done, I pulled my panties back up. He told me not to tell anybody and then ran away.

It took me a long time to get home, because my foot had become swollen from standing alongside the fence for so long. When I got home, no one ever asked where I had been. No one cared. I buried the devastation I felt within, never mentioning it to anyone.

After that incident, I walked to school every day wondering if that boy was going to attack me again. I would imagine I was Wonder Woman. Wonder Woman was all that I had to believe in. She was my hero. *He couldn't catch me then,* I thought.

My sister, my cousin, and I had a secret place located under

Grandmomma's house. This was *our* secret place, and no one could hurt us there. It was just big enough for us kids to feel safe and protected.

Sometimes, we made capes out of Grandmomma's white sheets and tied them around our necks. I drew "WW" for Wonder Woman on my cape. Sonya drew "SW" for Superwoman on hers. She imagined she was fighting the bad guys by tying them up with invisible ropes. James put the letters "SM" for Superman on his cape, and he was going to freeze the monsters with his powerful eyes, stopping them dead in their tracks. Together, we were the Super Friends.

I would twirl around and around with my cape on, faster and faster, just to feel the breeze zoom by my tiny body; believing whole-heartedly I would turn into this beautiful, powerful Wonder Woman. This way, I could fight off that big boy that did *it* to me. I could fly away from there and find a new home. Maybe people would think I was pretty instead of ugly. Maybe they wouldn't see all the scars on my body from switches and gem belts. My hair would be straight, long, and silky—instead of short, kinky and nappy. I could wear my hair in a long ponytail, with Shirley Temple curls, and even bows and ribbons. I never wore bows and ribbons in my hair.

This was the way I temporarily escaped the horrible conditions in which I was living. Something deep in my core told me the things that were being done to us was wrong—but I thought that things would never change and that this was the way life was going to be for us.

One day, during our impersonations of the Super Friends, we decided to climb the biggest tree in the backyard to test our super powers. James went first because he was Superman. He told us Superman went first. Sonya and I stood back and watched him climb the giant tree. He stood on a limb and took a leap. To our childish amazement, he didn't transform into a super being that could fly. Instead, he fell and hit the ground head first. Sonya and I started screaming and crying out for Grandmomma to come and help him. He was rushed to the hospital and had to get stitches in his head.

When Grandmomma found out we used her white sheets, we all got whippings. With each lash, my reality became clearer. My tears were not caused by the pain of the belt but by the realization that we didn't have super powers and could not change our present circumstances.

One day, Grandmomma overheard us talking about our uncles doing *it* to us. She asked us what we were talking about and we were afraid to tell her. After a lot of begging, pleading, and threatening of a "whooping," we finally broke down and told her what happened. She was infuriated. By that time, only one of our three uncles still lived at the house.

The youngest of my uncles dated a woman, which whom he constantly fought. One evening after a fight, she called her brothers and told them he had attacked her. Her brothers hunted him down and shot my uncle with a sawed-off shotgun. The blast from the gun blew a hole through his neck. He died instantly. I remember Granddaddy grabbing his gun and going to retaliate, but I can't remember the funeral or feeling remorse for his death. I could feel no natural grief about his sudden death because nothing about my relationship with him had ever been natural.

Meanwhile, the middle uncle had been tried and convicted of raping a young woman in the neighborhood. That's all we overheard my grandmomma say. He went to prison for a short time.

She let us whip the only remaining uncle with sticks for revenge. We also got "whooped," but for a different reason. We were whooped just to make sure this dirty little secret never left the house. After that, Grandmomma never mentioned it again.

Momma 5

Around the age of six, I awoke one morning with severe discomfort between my legs. My panties were always wet, but I never had any severe itching or burning. This day, I couldn't even walk normally. I walked to school gap-legged because my thighs were so raw and chafed. Through my youthful reasoning, I deduced that it was because I wet the bed so much. Momma was in and out of our lives during this time. She took me to the doctor and he said I had syphilis. That was when she begged me to tell her what happened. I was terrified and wouldn't tell her. Family Services almost took us away.

Sonya and I eventually told her it was my uncles who did *it* to us and what happened to us in her absence. She was furious and confronted Grandmomma. Then, she packed up our things and took us away from Grandmomma's house. We didn't know Momma had already found a place for us to live. It was an old raggedy house she called "Baby Elephant House."

"Baby Elephant" was the nickname of someone Momma knew who lived in the house prior to us. Since Momma knew the owner, she didn't have to pay rent; however, the house had no running water. We had to lug buckets of water from an outside hydrant to bathe and cook. Being that the house had an outside toilet, we had to cut wood for the fireplace to keep warm.

At first, moving in with my momma was somewhat of a relief. We really believed we had escaped the sexual torment we had grown to expect. Although we no longer had to live at Grandmomma's house, we still had to walk there after school. We had no reprieve from the sexual abuse.

We thought because Momma was taking us with her—it meant she was ready to be the world's greatest momma. Instead, we were constantly reminded of how much she never wanted us. We were looking for love and acceptance, and instead we got rage and resentment. We repeatedly heard words like, *"You oughtta' be glad I brought you in this world. I wish I never had you!"* She would say, *"I wish I had flushed you down the toilet. . ."* or *"I wish you had died."*

We were called bitches, whores, and whatever else came to her ailing mind. We never knew when she was going to snap.

Living with Momma was hard. We had learned to expect the worst from the world but had put great expectations on her. We had concocted a fantasy of what life would be like with her—believing she was the missing piece that would make all of our troubles a distant memory. Hearing her say those things to us was at times worse than the abuse we suffered at Grandmomma's house.

Every callous utterance from her mouth ripped right through my heart, and wiped out the fantasy life I had imagined. I only wanted her to hold me, and tell me that she loved me. I wanted her to tell me I was pretty and smart. I wanted her to build up what had been taken away from me. I wanted her to help me see what had been lost and to show me my value and tell me I had the potential to be anything I wanted to be. I just wanted her to be my momma.

Sometimes, Momma could drink a fifth of liquor a day. Then, she would go to sleep, wake up, and knock back another one. When she drank, things got worse. She acted like a fool. She would pull up her dress, slap her butt, and tell everybody to kiss *it.*

We watched Momma fight all the time, too. She fought her sisters, her boyfriends, and other women. She believed in fighting and always told us to fight. If we didn't, she would "whoop" us and make us go back to face the battle from which we had run.

One day, some children from the projects jumped on Sonya, James, and me. We ran home crying and scared, but Momma beat us, and then made us go back to fight. She would say, *"You better pick up a stick or brick, knock the hell out of 'em, and haul ass!"* In a sense, that was the way of the street and the norm in the 'hood. It didn't matter if we won the fight—what mattered was that we fought back.

******

Eventually, my uncle was released from prison. I am not sure if he was on probation or parole. We had moved to a better place; a two-bedroom apartment a good distance from Grandmomma's house. He found out we were living there and would visit us frequently.

If Momma happened to be drunk and unconscious, my uncle would come into our room and sexually abuse us. We locked our door, but we knew as soon as Momma passed out, he was going to come back for one of us. Sonya would climb into the bed with me and hold me tight. We would lie silently in the dark and listen to him pick the lock with a butter knife—or whatever object he could find. We would watch the knob slowly twist and turn, as though he thought we were asleep and didn't want to wake us. Once he had gained entry into the room, he would choose one of us. At times, Sonya would sacrifice herself for me by pleading, *"Please, don't take my little sister, take me instead."* Most of the time, he would take one of us to the bathroom and do his thing, while the other one would just lie in the bed; too afraid to watch; too afraid to cry; and too afraid to even move. After he was done, he would close the door behind him without waking Momma.

******

Momma would get so drunk; from time to time, she would walk home late at night and pretend she could fly—spreading her arms like wings and turning around and around. One particular night, she was so intoxicated that she couldn't walk home. Sonya and I found a grocery cart nearby. We put Momma in it and pushed her home. On the way, we lost our grip and control of the cart, causing it to roll downhill. Momma fell out the cart and into the street.

Another time, when Momma was too drunk to walk home, the police drove up, while we begged her to stand up straight. We propped her up with our bodies—on either side—so the officers would not take her to jail. She was all we had. The thought of losing her was something we couldn't bear. Momma had been taken to jail so many times for fighting, we thought she would eventually go for killing someone. Or even worse, someone might kill her.

There were times when Momma would drink alone and act calm; almost sedated or depressed. Then there were times when she seemed insane with happiness, only to become violent all over again. Later in life, I realized that unlike some people who drink to run away from their feelings, Momma drank just to feel. I never knew if the alcohol made the demons in her mind better or worse.

One day, Momma left Sonya and me at home with her boyfriend. He asked us to get in the bed with him so we could play house. At this point in our lives, we had been molested so often, we knew exactly what his idea of "playing house" meant. I got in the bed with him but Sonya didn't. He started to pull down my pants and put his fingers in my panties. My sister came into the room, got me out of the bed, and told him to leave me alone. We went into our bedroom and locked the door. I was scared, but if he had decided to open that door, I knew Sonya was prepared for a fight.

The next day, we told Momma what happened. She snapped, as if she had a personal memory of something just as vile. At the time, he wasn't there, so Momma made us hunt for him. We didn't have a car back then; therefore, we walked a long distance doing so. We finally found him at his momma's house. Momma confronted him, and they argued for a long time. As she turned to walk away from him, he picked up a 2 x 4 piece of wood, and hit her in the back of the head.

For a moment, the world stopped and fear gripped my lungs; not fear that my momma was hurt—because she didn't even blink. It was the fear of what was to come. I feared for his life. I knew he had angered and awakened the beast within her. Momma picked up an empty Thunderbird wine bottle, broke it, and slit his throat from ear to ear. She walked away and never looked back. On the other hand, I looked behind and saw the flashing lights of the ambulance as they arrived on the scene. Quite honestly, there were mixed emotions inside me. The amount of blood and tissue coming from his neck made me feel sorry for him. I hoped he wouldn't die; however, there was a part of me that felt for the first time that Momma cared about us and that felt good. To know that she would risk going to jail for us meant a lot. He survived—and later on—she took care of him when he developed cancer of the throat. She had to feed him from a tube. I guess she felt responsible. As time went by, they parted ways and he later died from cancer.

Momma didn't always fight for us. One night, around the age of 17, I was awakened by a tall, slim, naked man. He managed to pick my bedroom lock to come in and sexually assault me. He happened to be my momma's boyfriend at the time. I woke up screaming to a man down on his knees, vigorously caressing his penis over me. My naked momma ran in the room and yelled, *"What the hell is going on?"*

I told her he was on his knees, feeling me all over my body and touching his penis. Momma was furious and went off on me. She slapped me and told me he was her man and that it all was my fault. I was devastated. I cried and begged her to protect me. She later kicked me out of the house with nowhere to go. I went to my next door neighbor's house and stayed with her for a couple of days—until Momma finally got tired of the boyfriend and put him out. She told me to come back home as if nothing ever happened. We never talked about it again.

******

We didn't have birthday parties or even a cake. I never had a *Barbie* doll or an *Easy Bake Oven;* nevertheless, Momma always made sure we had somewhere to live. She always reminded us how lucky we were to have a roof over our head.

We had Section Eight housing, which made it easier for us to move often. We only had to sign a one-year lease. If Momma got tired of where we were living, she put her notice in to Section Eight and moved.

Momma eventually went to a community college and took some cooking courses. She loved cooking and was the best cook in the world—even better than Grandmomma. Those were the two things she provided for us: a place to stay and food to eat. She would bake and sell all kinds of pies and cakes. Her specialties were red velvet cake, sweet potato pie, and pecan pie. She taught us how to cook and made us help her in the kitchen.

She was different when she was cooking and easier to be around. We didn't always talk about anything important, but we knew that it was a moment when all her defenses were down. As I entered into my adolescent years, all the kids in the neighborhood would come to eat at our house despite being afraid of Momma.

My momma didn't have many friends, and I never saw her hang out with many women. She started sending us to the same church my grandmomma, granddaddy, and aunts attended every Sunday. We would come home to tell her about the service and beg her to go with us that next Sunday. Eventually, she joined the church. Life got much easier. She was a much better person. She was still angry and unhappy, but there were more pleasant moments.

Momma never talked about her life or the things that bothered her. Instead, she kept it bottled up inside. Whenever she left the church, Momma would start drinking again. It wasn't long after before the fighting and emotional abuse would resume. We prayed for her return to church—so we would have some relief.

PART 2

THE ADOLESCENT YEARS

HIGH SCHOOL

Throughout my adolescence, Momma was heavily into going to church. Growing up in the Holiness Church wasn't easy for Sonya and me. As our bodies started to blossom during our pre-teen years, we wanted to look like the girls in our age group.

Our church pastor was the most powerful woman I had ever known. She had zero tolerance for any kind of sin; if you sinned, you were surely going straight to hell. She was especially tough on children. We couldn't wear certain clothes, go to the movies or buy, sing or listen to any music that wasn't gospel. We couldn't wear pants, makeup, or jewelry. We had to wear our skirts and dresses long enough to cover the middle of our calves. Because of this, we were badly teased in school. We were called names like *sanctified woman*, *little nasty*, *big nasty*, *bald-headed*, *voodoo*, and too many other taunts to remember.

I recall walking home from school and being teased by the boys in the neighborhood. All I wanted was to look like all the other girls. I didn't have to be popular. I just needed to fit in.

By the time I was in middle school, it seemed like all I did was go to church. I loved going to church and learning about the Bible. We spent all day in church on Sundays, and then on Tuesday and Friday nights. All day Saturday was spent in choir practice. That seemed like a lot.

At the end of my eighth grade year, Momma moved to another part of town. Changing schools was devastating to me because I had to make new friends; even though, I was excited about starting high school.

Momma worked as a maid "Over the Mountain" three days each week. "Over the Mountain" was the ghetto phrase we used to describe the wealthy neighborhoods. Public transportation didn't travel into the upper-class neighborhoods; therefore, Momma would have to get picked up by the person she was working for at the time. I remember Momma would sometimes take Sonya and me to several of the massive, stunning, three-story homes she cleaned. The homes had large bedrooms and bathrooms, beautiful furniture, lots of bookcases, wooden staircases, high ceilings, and state-of-the-art swimming pools. Some of these homes even had three-car garages. The people who lived there always treated us well. They would send us designer clothes their children no longer wanted or had outgrown. We were very poor.

School clothing for Sonya and me was a joke. Once Momma gave us $10 apiece, and we went to the thrift store to buy clothes for school. Other times, we would go to clothing banks. We felt fortunate when Momma brought us hand-me-downs from her wealthy, white employers.

Besides Momma giving us a few dollars here and there for school clothes and bringing used clothes from work, we had no other way of clothing ourselves. If we asked Momma for name-brand clothes or shoes, or needed bras or panties, she would explain how hard she worked every day just to keep a roof over our heads and food on the table. We should be grateful for that—she would say. It was left up to us to get the things we needed the best way we could.

I started shoplifting to get whatever I needed to blend in with the crowd. I was amazed at how easy it was to get away with the stolen goods and got a thrill from it. Sometimes, Momma would ask me where I got some of the new, expensive clothes. I would tell her someone gave them to me or that I was borrowing them from a friend. Even though, I knew she realized I was stealing from the store. Every now and then, she would say to me—*"You better not be putting your hands on those people's stuff in them stores!"*

Along with *my* new, stolen clothesthere came a sense of pride. I started feeling better about myself. By dressing and looking like the other girls at school, I even got some attention from the boys. This gave me a little more confidence and I felt like I fit in. I started hanging out with some of the popular girls and began getting invited to social outings like the skating rink, house parties, clubs, and school events. This was just what I wanted and needed.

I started going to school every day; although, I was late most of the time. I loved school. I was making new friends and doing well academically. I was happy and finally felt like I belonged somewhere; like I was accepted. I grew more outgoing and confident. I was more vocal, too; not only because I wanted people to look at me, but for the first time, I truly didn't mind it at all.

MY FIRST LOVE

When I was about 14 years old, I was enthralled by a boy named Henry who lived down the street. He was 16, had a dark Hershey's chocolate complexion, and long, naturally curly hair. His small frame and muscular build made him look so fine. When he walked down the street shirtless, it was like he owned it. He strutted as the sun's rays reflected on his six-pack. I adored him.

One day, when I was playing with my friends, he walked up and kissed me on the cheek. I was mesmerized. He was considered a thug in the community—which, of course, made him even more attractive—so I didn't tell anyone about him. I was also afraid of what my momma and the people in the church would think if they ever found out I liked him. He reminded me of one of the singers from the early 80's R&B group, *Ready for the World*. I found it hard to breathe, whenever I saw him. My stomach would twist and roll with butterflies, my mouth would salivate, and my lips would smolder with passion and desire. All the girls liked Henry, but I was in love.

Another day, as I was playing in an abandoned house next door to his home, he walked in. My heart began to flutter and beat so fast, I thought I was going into cardiac arrest. He laid me down on the floor and kissed me. My heart skipped a beat and my knees weakened. I was captivated. He slowly started pulling up my favorite pink skirt. I said no, but he begged me to let him do *it* to me. After a brief tug-of-war, I got away from him and ran home like Lindsay Wagner in the *Bionic Woman*.

I was terrified of what Momma would think if she found out what I was doing.

Like any other teenaged girl, I knew I was too young to have sex. There was always the possibility I could get pregnant or contract a sexually-transmitted disease. Growing up in the Holiness Church, which held the strict belief that sex before marriage was fornication in God's eyes—didn't help either. I was terrified of what my pastor would think of me. I was very active in church. I sang in the choir and was an usher every Sunday. I also baby-sat for most of the church members.

I valued my pastor's teaching and believed I would burn in hell for my sins. After all, my momma never really told me about sex. She always said, *"Keep your dress down and your panties up."* Momma didn't like Henry. Come to think of it, Momma didn't like anybody, especially boys.

******

When I was a freshman in high school, all the cool girls—the ones I thought were cool—spoke comfortably about how they were *doin' it* with their boyfriends. This was exciting to me. Everybody was *doin' it*, except me. My closest friend, Tanita, had already done it, and

I wanted to be just like her. I constantly daydreamed about *doin' it* with Henry.

I wanted to fit in. I wanted to be like all the other girls. I wanted so badly to know what it *really* felt like to make love. Other than what I had seen on TV, and had learned from the streets, my only experiences with sex were the horrifying memories of my uncles on top of me; hurting me, violating me. That wasn't sex. It was abuse. It was rape.

I had blocked all the sexual abuse out of my mind, at this time in my life. It was like it never happened to me. I didn't even think about it—nor did I talk about it to anyone. Like most teenagers, I wanted my first sexual experience to be with someone special.

******

One evening, we were in Henry's bedroom. He laid me down on the bed. It was dark and the deejay was playing love songs on the radio. I remember my favorites: Ready for the World's *Let Me Love You Down* and Prince's *Purple Rain*. At last, I was in the arms of someone I desired. I was nervous, but I wanted him.

He whispered four words, "I will be gentle." My brain and tongue seemed disconnected and I couldn't say a word. And then, it happened. I had finally done it with someone I loved. For the first time, I wasn't forced, held down, choked, or tied up. I didn't have to be coerced to do something I didn't want to do. My clothes weren't ripped off, my head wasn't beaten against the floor, and I wasn't consumed with fear. The feeling was incredible!

Tears of enthusiasm rolled down my face. I had never experienced a man on top of me; a man I wanted to be there. I closed my eyes tightly, while his hands caressed my trembling body. His lips passionately touched mine and his penis gently penetrated my vagina. The entire experience only lasted for a few minutes but it seemed like a lifetime. I had reached pure ecstasy for the first time in my life.

We were both afraid someone would come in the room and bust us. As quickly as it was over, I jumped up, pulling up my panties and pushing down my skirt. I ran all the way home skipping and jumping, without stopping to catch my breath.

With teenage hormones flaring, we spent months *bumpin'* and *grindin'* in secret places. I had done it… *and I liked it.* It felt good. I felt good. *Did that mean that I wasn't a virgin anymore?* Or because of the sexual abuse, did it mean that I wasn't a virgin from the start? I was confused. Of course, I knew I had never felt these emotions with my uncles. This was different. It was beautiful, soft, and succulent. It was love.

For the next six years, on and off, I was foolishly in love with Henry. He was the love of my life. I was sprung! I sacrificed every-thing for him. I didn't care about anything or anyone. I didn't care about going to school or church. All I cared about was being with him. He gave me a kind of freedom from my abusive past, but he never claimed me. He only saw me at night. He never took me out. He never really spent any time with me, except for sex. He would see me walking down the street and would barely speak to me. This hurt. I would write him long letters expressing my love for him and desperately asking him to love me; to be with me.

Then I heard he got another girl pregnant. I was devastated. I hated him for stomping my heart into a million pieces, but I couldn't stay away from him. I couldn't eat, sleep, or even go to school. I just wanted to die. I would sneak out of the house in the middle of the night just to see him. I would call his house all hours of the night, hoping he would answer. If his momma answered, I would hang up.

That infuriated her. Sometimes, she would call me back and cuss me out for waking her up.

On one of the many mornings I crept out of the house to meet Henry, we got in his car and parked in his backyard. My momma woke up and saw I was missing. She walked around to his house and woke up his momma. They both started looking for us. They found us in the car and started banging on the window. I had my head lying on his lap, while we were talking. Thank God we weren't doing anything, but we got cussed out. My momma knocked the hell out of me and made me go home. Of course, that didn't stop us. We were like Romeo and Juliet. We were constantly sneaking off together. They just got used to it. Eventually, my momma allowed him to come to the house to visit me.

Over a period of time, I got tired of being in the shadows. I told him how I felt about the way he treated me. He apologized and we officially became a couple. Finally, after all the years of me chasing him, loving him, crying over him, and aching from a broken heart, he confessed his true love for me. I wasn't a secret anymore. Everybody knew we were a couple; however, that didn't last long.

HIGH SCHOOL DROPOUT

During my sophomore year, I began to lose interest in school. My relationship with Henry was a big distraction and emotionally draining, and I wasn't able to focus on schoolwork. By the time I entered the 11th grade, I had already stopped studying. I had stopped going to classes and never read or brought my textbooks home. My report card was the proof. I received Ds and Fs in almost every class.

I started sneaking around behind Momma's back and wearing jeans, makeup, and jewelry. I would change my clothes in the alley behind my apartment before going inside, hiding my pants in the closet or at my friends' houses.

During my junior year, I found a job making $75.00 each week at a popular restaurant located in Five Points West. It was close enough to walk back and forth from home. I never had any money, so working was exciting to me. I would get my paycheck and walk to the liquor store to cash it. Then, I would walk to the very store I got caught stealing from and stuff my purse with clothes. I don't know why I kept stealing when I had money. But I guess buying what I wanted didn't make sense to me. *Why pay for something when I could steal it?* I worked every day and even late nights. I just wanted to make money. It felt good cashing checks with my name on them.

Momma didn't ask me for too much money. She only requested that I pay the telephone bill, since I used the phone all the time. I got completely caught up in working and buying myself underclothes and other girly things. All my home girls at school had jobs and we shopped at the mall together. I had all the latest fashions: *Coca-Cola* and *Pepsi* shirts, sweater skirts, leg warmers, *Chic* jeans, *Gloria Vanderbilt*, and *Guess*.

I had just given up on school. I had no role model in my life. I figured—my momma and sister had dropped out of school, so why shouldn't I drop out? After all, Momma didn't make it mandatory for us to graduate from high school and there was never any talk about college. Still, with that in mind, I knew that education was important and I had no good reason to drop out of school. I wasn't pregnant, although some of my friends had gotten pregnant. I was *doin' it* just as much as they were. I was just lucky. I wasn't dumb. I just didn't care. I had lost every desire to go to school. I was in the 11th grade and still taking 10th grade classes because I had flunked several classes the year before. At the end of the school year, I went to school to gather my personal belongings. My history teacher saw me in the hallway and asked me to retake my final test so he could give me a passing grade. I told him I would be back the next morning to retake the test. I never went back.

Momma never questioned me about dropping out of school. She never asked me why nor did she tell me to go back to school. In fact, no one ever said to me, "Take your ass back to school." If somebody had, then maybe, just maybe, I would not have dropped out and continued my family's cycle.

PART 3

THE STREETS

THE ROADS TO SELF-DESTRUCTION

After dropping out of high school at 17, I started working at restaurants that paid about $3.25 an hour. From there, I moved on to warehouses. It wasn't hard for me to go down the road to self-destruction because I lived in the heart of the ghetto right next door to a dope house. This was the early 80's when crack cocaine erupted on the scene. The dope house was hot and all my "homies" sold crack rocks out of the apartment. This was in extreme contrast to the way Momma made us live. If it didn't have anything to do with God, Momma wasn't havin' it. Now here were all these thugs living next door to us selling drugs. Momma hated all the traffic, loud music, parties, and women going to and from the apartment at all times of the day and night.

I loved it. I got the chance to hang out with a new crowd. They gave me a different kind of attention. They looked out for me. They gave me money to cook, wash, and clean up for them. They wouldn't dare let another dude step up to me. They would run him off. Doing so strengthened their chances of getting with me first.

They would compete with each other by being the first to ask me out or pick me up from work. They were extra nice to Momma, gave me money, took me out to eat, and did everything guys do to get a woman's attention. They saw that I was an insecure little girl, but my body had transformed into a woman's. My flat stomach, long legs, small waistline, and big booty made them chase after me. I always had a "Brick House" shape, and Momma made sure to keep it covered. I couldn't go to church looking like a hussy. This was something new and exciting for me; someone cute, fly, and rich was asking me my name? *Huh?*

Henry and I had played the break-up and make-up game so many times that I could feel the relationship about to end. I held on because I was in love mostly for sentimental reasons. He was my first and someone I wanted to be with. As time went on, our relationship transformed and our feelings toward each other changed. During our breakups, I began to see other men who were interested. They were men who I thought were powerful and gave me more than attention. They showered me with money and gifts. Ultimately, my interest began to shift. It hurt every time Henry and I broke up, but mostly, because I wasn't ready to let go.

There was one charming, irresistible dealer who sold drugs out of the apartment next door. Junior was one of the smoothest men I had ever met. He had a swagger that could charm any woman. He had a convincing conversation and wasted no time trying to get in my panties. He was slick as "Rick." He constantly chased me, asking me out. He tried seducing me by taking me to work and picking me up. He would give me money to buy clothes and bring me small gifts. Junior had a sharp sports car with a spoiler and customized leather seats with his initials carved in them. He was the biggest baller on the block. He had everybody working for him. He was definitely a businessman. He had plenty of women running in and out of the apartment looking for him. He was good to all of his women and had many children. Sometimes, he had two or three babies on the way at one time. He lived the life of a womanizer and lived it with fervor. He had a record shop, a few houses, and more apartments he used to peddle his drugs. He was a big spender and carried large amounts of money around all the time. He asked if I wanted to go to Atlanta to see Keith Sweat in concert. I had never been outside of Alabama—I was flabbergasted! He made me feel special.

Junior introduced me to selling drugs, so that I could make some fast money. Since I hung out next door all the time, I soon learned how to cook, cut, and bag crack cocaine. I was given a gun and a beeper. My street name was "Booty," and I had become an official dope girl. I was out of control and living the life.

I was pulling shifts in the dope house around the clock. Momma finally put me out, so I started living in hotels. Of course, I could have gone home; however, that was the first time in my life I was able to do what I wanted... *and it felt good.*

My boys spent all kinds of money on Moët, food, and clothes. I was 18 with a fake ID I got from *Newberry's*, the store everybody went to for fake identification cards. They never worked, because all the club owners were aware of the fakes. In any case, because of their greed to make money, they always let us in.

I was deep into the clubs, the "bling-bling," the 20-inch rims, money, customized cars, and "ballers." I started hanging at the club at least three nights per week. I had found another addiction. I got there the best way I could. I would get dropped off by strangers, cabs, friends or any means necessary. I was living the fast life, hanging out in the club until sunrise.

I became a regular; everybody knew me. I started a dangerous cycle of meeting, dating, and sleeping with (I should say trickin') dope men. I wanted money and power. I didn't care if he was married or not. I didn't care about his name, age, or looks. All I cared about was how much money he had and how much I was going to get.

My club buddies and I were unstoppable. I woke up and laid down to go to the clubs, to buy, steal, or buy and steal an outfit, to get my nails done and my weave hooked up. I had to look good. I had to have the latest name brand, go to all the hottest parties, and be seen with the player of players. It was just a part of being in the game. I was a hard core bitch. I had no love for any man. I played dangerous games. I would see who I wanted when I wanted. If the dude I was with didn't like it, he either dealt with it or he got kicked to the curb.

BABY BOY

It wasn't long before I caught a man's attention. I went to the same club every week and always saw Chris there with plenty of women in his face. He drove a two-toned gold Corvette and was definitely a "baller." He was of average height, wore fresh clothes, and had a James Brown perm. He would constantly stare at me. He bought me drinks and we danced a few times.

One night Chris chased me until I finally gave in and went to breakfast with him. He was sort of cute, but my motives were the same as with all of the men who tried to be with me. There was no love. Sex was like a business, "No money, no honey." My agenda was all about what they could do for me.

Well, this time, I got played. I ended up staying at his place for about three days. He had a little shack behind his auntie's house. Everybody called it the Little House on the Prairie. I had heard about this spot from some of the girls from the club who had been there. The house had no phone and no bathroom.

To use the bathroom, guests had to go to his aunt's house. This was a little spot for him and some of his boys to hang out.

During those three days I had no clean clothes, no toothbrush, no feminine products, and worst of all, no birth control pills. I had left them at home in another purse by mistake. Now that I think about it, I could have left. I wasn't held there against my will, although every day I begged him to take me home. I was worried about Momma not hearing from me. Because I was so naïve, I did nothing to escape. After all, I was diggin' him and I thought he was diggin' me, too. I felt like it was my fault I was there. If I hadn't gotten in the car, I would not have been in that situation. I did know that I would never go anywhere with him again once I got out of there. During the day we would talk, laugh, watch movies, listen to the radio, eat, and hang out. During the night, we had sex until morning. I had taken birth control pills faithfully since I was 16 and never missed a day, but one lapse is all it took.

******

"It's your turn!" My friends teased as I walked with the nurse back to the Family Planning Department to take my pregnancy test.

After I sat and waited for a while, the nurse called me back to her station. "Well," she said, "your test is positive. Now what are you going to do?"

I will never forget the nurse asking all of us to come into her office to talk about teenage pregnancy and prevention. She explained my options: I could have an abortion or give my baby up for adoption. I knew that those were not choices for me. Momma wouldn't let me do something like that. The church taught us that abortion was a sin. The nurse was talking but I couldn't hear what she was saying.

This couldn't be real. Was this actually happening to me? I was 19 and devastated. I was shocked that I was pregnant. I had gotten away with being promiscuous with Henry for three years without a single pregnancy scare. I wasn't even sure who the daddy was. Was it Henry or Chris? I had an idea the baby wasn't Henry's, but I wanted it to be.

I wasn't too nervous about telling my mother. I knew she didn't care enough to be disappointed. Her main concern would be another mouth to feed. I went home and gave my mother the pregnancy test with the pink plus sign. She said, "You need to go sign up for food stamps, housing, and welfare. I will help you with one baby but if you get another one, you're on your own." That was it. That was all she said.

******

Throughout my entire pregnancy I managed to slow down. I didn't tell many people I was pregnant, but of course the news got out. I was about six months along when I told Henry that I was pregnant and he might not be the daddy. I told him all about what happened with the other man. I never told Chris, but he heard about it. He came over one day and asked if it was his baby. I said no and that was the end of it.

My water broke at home and I had no one to help me. My next-door neighbor took me to the hospital where I delivered a breech baby boy by Caesarean section, all alone. I looked at my handsome, tiny son, RaShod, only five pounds and six ounces, and felt scared and alone. I had no blue balloons that read: *Congratulations, it's a boy!* There were no flowers, no cards, no friends, and no "baby daddy." I can remember the pain I felt having a baby alone. There was such terrible pain from the contractions, and worse pain from the absence of the baby's father and Momma. I kept thinking—*This is supposed to be the happiest moment in my life. I am bringing a life into the world. I'm not supposed to be here doing this by myself. I'm not supposed to be like my momma. I'm not supposed to have a fatherless child.* I wanted to be happy. I wanted to feel the magic of motherhood. I found myself yet again continuing my family's cycle.

I watched the girl next to me when her family came in with balloons and flowers. They saw me watching and I think they saw the longing on my face. They asked where my family was. I told them nobody came and they tried to make me feel better. It wasn't the same.

"I'll see you next year," the nurse said as she rolled my wheelchair to the front door of the hospital after discharging us. The nurse's words stunned me. I knew, at that moment, I was not a BREEDER. No, no, she was not going to see me again for a very long time.

THE VISION:
RUN FOR YOUR LIFE

I had long stopped attending church by the time I got pregnant with RaShod. After his birth, every now and then I would go to church and take the baby for everyone to see. I would always walk to the altar to ask for prayer and forgiveness for my sins. I never left church without speaking to Mother, my pastor, and telling her I would come back to God soon. But I was enjoying ripping and running the streets. I didn't have to go to church three times every week. I didn't have to sing in the choir anymore. I didn't have to wear long dresses and skirts.

I loved wearing makeup, tight jeans, and short dresses. I didn't have to feel guilty anymore when I hooked up with one of my boys. Momma was still going to church but slowly losing interest as usual. Mother would always ask all of us children who had drifted away from the church and from God to come back and repent before God before it was too late. She would send messages through Momma to tell me to get back in the church while I still had a chance. She got really sick and was admitted to the hospital. Everybody visited her except some of the other children who had left the church and me.

When Momma visited Mother in the hospital, Mother told her she wanted to see me because God had given her a warning about me. Momma came home and gave me the message. I didn't want to go to the hospital to hear what she had to tell me. I was scared to face the truth, to hear her say I was a sinner. I wasn't ready to stop living the life I was living and I didn't want to be judged.

As soon as I made up my mind to finally go visit my pastor, I got word she had died. Oh, my God, Mother died before I could get the chance to hear what she had to tell me; what God had to tell me. What did this mean? What had I done? I was distraught. I was so hurt, I cried and cried for months. Was I a bad person? Was I doomed for hell? God knew I loved my pastor. After all, she was about the only positive role model I had ever had in my life. I went into a depression and mourned her death every day.

One night, I was asleep and had a vision that I was standing around a group of people, some familiar and some strangers. I heard everybody talking about a girl who had died. They wanted to know who this strange girl was. What happened to her? I was standing around trying to see this girl that lay on the ambulance gurney with a white sheet pulled over her body. I couldn't see her face. I could only see the back of her head and her hair. Suddenly, I realized the girl was me! I wore my hair the exact same way at the time of the vision. I knew it was me. I began to cry out loud, "Oh, my God, that's me. Please God, don't let me die a sinner. I need you. Help me, save me."

I started to run as fast as I could. I had to beat the ambulance to the hospital before they pronounced, me, the girl on the stretcher dead. I knew if that girl died before repenting for her sins, I would then die along with her. I was not sure whether it would be a physical death or a spiritual death. As the ambulance took off, I began to run next to it. It was too late. I didn't make it in time. They pronounced the girl dead. The next thing I saw was the hearse taking her body to the same church I had served God in all my life until now. I began to run in the street next to the hearse. Cars were honking at me and people were yelling, "Get your ass out of the street, fool. Are you crazy?"

I was running for my life, crying and begging God not to let me die. "I ain't ready to die! Please, give me another chance."

As the hearse pulled up to the church, they slowly rolled the body inside. I could see everybody was crying. I ran past the body and busted through the big stained-glass church doors, sprinting straight to the altar. I saw a beautiful woman with wings wearing a pure white robe. It was Mother. She came back to tell me that God wanted her to tell me to run for my life. She said, "Johnnetta, come to Mother. Mother loves you. Run... run for your life before it is too late."

I ran into her arms, crying and yelling, "Please forgive me. I am so sorry for not coming to the hospital." I fell on my weary knees and started crying profusely. "Please forgive me, Jesus. Help me, Jesus. Save me from my sins, Jesus. Please don't let me die. Give me one more chance."

When I awoke, I was petrified. I was soaking wet from sweating and crying. It was over. I finally got closure. I finally understood what God wanted her to tell me. Now, I know why God spared my life for all these years. I know why I am running for my life... to save other lives with the same story as mine.

WANNA BE A GOOD MOMMA

I was now somebody's momma. How was this going to affect my life? Would I still be able to have fun, and do the things that I had found so captivating? My priorities were jumbled. I knew I wanted to be a better mother than the one I had, but I was still young, and I needed to feel like myself. I wasn't ready to be someone's momma.

Two weeks after I gave birth, I was back on the scene. I was partying at the same club. I was nearly 20 years old. I had a baby by a dope man I barely knew, and who denied my child from the first moment he saw him. I had no job, no education, and no baby daddy. Henry wasn't around anymore. He forgave me but moved on with his life.

RaShod was a good baby and so handsome. He was very quiet and reserved. Sometimes it was hard to tell when he was in the room.

He had no problem learning anything, except telling time. When he was one year old, he learned how to use the potty on his second attempt. He was really short and slim for his age and so quiet, we hardly knew he was in the room.

Momma was a full-time baby-sitter; she watched RaShod at night while I worked and went out. She was good to him and let us live with her. She was still a no-nonsense woman and didn't let me get away with too much.

One night, I was at the club and some of my girls came running inside yelling, "Yo Momma is outside!" I thought, I didn't hear them right. Momma had driven to the club, put RaShod on the hood of his dad's car wearing nothing but a diaper and left. She had enough and didn't want to watch him that night for some reason or another. I was stuck outside the club, looking like a fool, holding my baby in his diaper. Thankfully, one of my "homies" brought us home.

******

RaShod was always mature for his age. When he was in the first grade, I visited his classroom. The teacher asked all the students what they wanted to be when they grew up. After the students picked doctors, lawyers, and nurses, RaShod shouted out, *"I want to be a security guard!"* He had run out of things to choose. It was so hard not to burst out laughing.

The teachers couldn't believe RaShod came from a one-parent household. They would send letters and notes addressed to Mr. and Mrs. McSwain. One evening, I arrived at the school for a parent conference and they asked if his father, my husband, would be attending. I said, "You're looking at both of them." The teacher shared how well-mannered, respectful, and nicely dressed RaShod was every day. He was a very polite child and everybody loved him.

He hardly ever got into trouble and only received a few whippings when he was little.

When he was 10 years old, a few days before Christmas, I came home and his TV was cracked and all the money from his piggybank was depleted. For hours, I asked him what happened. He stuck to his story that someone must have broken into the house, knocked his TV off the dresser, and stole his money out of his piggybank. I had bought him about $300 worth of Christmas gifts on Black Friday. We had so many toys that they were hidden in three commercial-sized black garbage bags. I really felt like Santa Claus, dragging those bags to my mid-size Mustang. Since I didn't believe his story, I threatened to call everyone he knew and tell them what he had done and take all his toys back to the mall if he didn't tell me the truth. He finally told me the truth and received the beat-down of his life for lying to me. The next day, he and I unwrapped every toy that belonged to him. We took them back to the mall and returned them toy by toy. He was more devastated about me telling everybody what he had done. He didn't care about the toys going back to the store. He wanted to protect his reputation as a good boy. That was truly a Christmas that the Grinch stole from RaShod. The only toys he received were the ones other family members gave him.

There were times when Rashod would ask me about his father and his family tree. I never lied to him and always told him the entire truth. When he asked if there was a Santa Claus, I said, "No. I am Santa Claus." When he asked me about the Tooth Fairy, I explained that I was the Tooth Fairy. When he asked me about his father, I told him, *"I made some mistakes and your father never owned up to being your father, but I am here. I am going to make sure you are loved and protected and I will try my best to raise you the best I can."*

GED

I was making $3.35 an hour at a popular restaurant in Five Points West. Neither Momma nor I had a car. Often I had to walk about 30 minutes one way to and from work. The restaurant stayed open 24 hours so when scheduled, I worked all three shifts. When I wasn't at work, I was preparing outfits to wear to the club. Some mornings I had to get up at 5 a.m. to get RaShod ready for daycare. He went to a daycare center a church member ran from her home. Sometimes I had to walk several blocks in the dark and cold to the daycare, carrying RaShod on my hip, in order to catch the bus to be at work at 7 a.m.

I wasn't prepared for parenthood at my age. At the time, welfare for one child was $88 per month, which wasn't enough money to take care of a baby. Besides, I didn't want to be on the welfare system. I didn't want those folks in my business. For some strange reason, I had the nerve to have a little pride. I knew flipping hamburgers for $3.35 an hour was not going to get me far, so I needed a high-school diploma. I was very ashamed of dropping out of high school and tired of lying about having a diploma on job applications. Everyone in my family had dropped out of high school and their lives offered proof of what happens to dropouts.

******

One day I was on the bus and saw a flier that read, "GED classes starting soon." I wrote down the contact information. The next day I called the number and spoke to a representative about the criteria for the GED program. She asked me some questions and made an appointment for the following day. I was excited about meeting her. I went the next day and filled out an application for the program. It was a state-run program funded through the Urban League. The program lasted 12 weeks and included a teacher that taught each part of the GED test, practice tests, books, all supplies, and a monthly stipend to help with bus fare and lunch. After I filled out the application, I learned I was eligible for the next session that was starting in a few months. I was so excited to be studying for my GED. I knew I couldn't continue through life without an education.

I started the program and was there every day, on time. I excelled in the program. I passed my entire practice test. I had to show up on test day at 7 a.m. sharp—one minute late meant disqualification from the test. I was there bright and early. I had eight hours to complete all five parts of the test. I remember watching my classmates complete their exams in record-breaking time. One by one, they finished their tests and trickled out of the room. I thought to myself, *I must be dumb because I am the last person still sitting here taking this test.* At 3 p.m., I was just completing my test. I turned it in to the administrator and left the room. Although I was exhausted, I felt as though I had done well.

A few weeks later, I received my results. I opened the envelope and read:

We regret to inform you that you did not score a passing grade on your GED test. We suggest you retake the parts of the test that received low scores.

I was so disappointed. I made a 44.5 on the test. I missed it by a half of one point. I had to make a 45 to pass the test, and they didn't round up the scores. I was happy that I passed the math and writing with flying colors, but I had to retake the Social Science part, which was the section I scored the least points. I only needed a few points to pass.

The same day I received the letter, I scheduled an appointment for my retest. I returned to take the test a few weeks later and was the only student there. In May of 1991, I received my test results. I opened the envelope and read: Congratulations! You passed the GED test.

Inside was my diploma. I was the only student that passed the test in a class of about 30.

At the graduation, I was chosen to speak at the ceremony. No one in my family bothered to show up.

Every Woman Needs
Her Own Kitchen

Momma told Sonya and me the very same thing her momma told her, "There's only one grown woman in this house. Every woman needs her own kitchen."

Momma eventually gave up her Section 8 housing. Sonya had gotten married and moved out. I was 20 and RaShod was one. Momma planned to move back to the same little yellow shotgun house we once lived in when I was about eight years old. It contained a small living room, one bedroom, a kitchen, and a very small bathroom.

Momma really did not want the baby and me following her to her new home. It was not that she didn't want us there. She just wanted to do her own thing for a change. She had so-called "raised" her children and she wanted to live her life on her terms. I could understand that. I didn't want to live with her anymore either. I didn't want to leave my 'hood.

I had met a young woman around my age that had recently moved into an upstairs apartment in our complex. She had just relocated from the other side of town and didn't like her new environment. She had three small children and was rather quiet. She didn't come outside much, but when she did, she always smiled and spoke to everyone. One day she came downstairs and knocked on the door to use the telephone. She saw RaShod and fell in love with him. She started to come down every day and we began a great friendship. I told her that Momma was moving and I didn't want to move. I asked if I could move upstairs into her two-bedroom apartment. This was my first attempt to try and live on my own. I moved my bed and some clothes into the room with her daughter. She was nice to me and we got along well. She was separated from her children's father and tried to see him every chance she got, but neither one of us had a car and he lived on the other side of town.

We lived on a busy street that attracted many drug dealers and wannabe "ballers," who cruised around in flashy cars with shiny rims and plenty of bass in the trunk. One day, my roommate wanted to see her ex-boyfriend real bad. She wasn't a bad-looking girl, so she attracted the attention of two guys who stopped their car when they saw her in the parking lot. She came and got me from the apartment and asked if I would ride with her to go to see her baby daddy on the other side of town. Thinking neither one of us should ride with two total strangers, I said yes anyway, got a baby-sitter, and jumped in the back seat of the car. As we rode, we carried on a decent conversation with both men. About 30 minutes later, we arrived at her baby daddy's house. She got out and yelled to me, "I'll be right back." She stayed in the house so long the driver got frustrated and started blowing the horn. She came back to the car and told me she was going to stay there and asked the driver if he could take me back home. He said no problem and drove off.

As he was driving, I noticed his demeanor changed from kind and friendly to weird and scary. He was driving in an entirely different direction from my apartment. I began to get nervous. I knew something wasn't right. However, I kept talking trying not to let on that I feared for my life. He noticed I was uneasy; I could see his big, wide, evil eyes looking at me in the rearview mirror. I knew that whatever he was going to try to do to me he had done before. He drove out by the airport where we used to party. It was always pitch dark and no one could see in the car. That's the reason everyone chose this spot to party. He drove through a dark path leading to tall grass and trees. I couldn't see anything but the lights coming in from the airplanes across the way. He parked deep in the grass where the car was invisible. My heart was pounding and I began to panic. He pulled out something from his pants. Seeing the metallic shine of the object, I realized immediately it was a gun. He said, "Bitch, pull your pants down and give me some pussy!" The other passenger was scared. He was trying to talk the crazed driver out of raping me.

I said, "Wait, I have to pee. Please let me get out so I can pee." I convinced him I needed to get out of the back seat to squat by the car. As soon as I got outside, I ran for my life. I ran through the tall grass, losing my sandals along the way. I was running on dirt, sticks, and gravel. I could see the lights from the car driving through the meadow, searching for me. I felt like a wild baby impala being chased by a pack of hungry African lions. I kept running blindly through the bushes, only to fall into a ditch of large, sharp rocks. One rock pierced the bone in my knee. Ignoring the excruciating pain in my knee and the blood pumping down my leg, I lay in the tall bushes for hours—afraid to breathe, afraid to scream, afraid to move.

After a while I didn't hear a sound, so I got up and limped through the bushes to the street until I found a house. I rapped on the door and a nice woman answered my knock. I asked her to call the police, saying someone had just tried to rape me at gunpoint. She called the police, helped me into the house, and cleaned my knee with alcohol. The police came and took me back home. I got home, ran some hot bath water, got in the tub and cried all night. I thought of what could have happened, what would have happened to RaShod. My choices and behavior were not good, and I had not really considered my son.

Later, my roommate came home and apologized profusely. We cried together. The next day I couldn't walk. My knee had a deep gash in it and was swollen to twice its normal size. I went to the emergency room and got a few stitches. I was so hurt and ashamed I couldn't tell anyone. Writing this now is the first time I've ever thought of telling anyone. It was one thing to be molested by my uncles but raped at gunpoint by two strange men in the middle of the night—I couldn't even think about it. I never saw those guys again. They knew where I lived, but I never saw them on my side of town. Maybe they thought I could remember their faces and press charges against them for attempted rape. I have to admit, I often wonder if they did that to another woman.

******

I started dating a notorious drug dealer who had a reputation for beating his women down if they got out of line or didn't do what he demanded. I knew him from being around the clubs and messing around with other women in the neighborhood. I saw him stomp his "baby momma" down in the street, as he left her there bleeding. But there was something about him that attracted me. It was his beautiful, smooth, extra-dark skin. He had deep dimples in his cheeks, a pearly white smile, and a body like L L Cool J. He was a thuggish, ruggish "N."

I knew he was dangerous and could beat me down at any time, but I liked him. He had a dope house behind my apartment complex, so he came over whenever he wanted. He mostly showed up unannounced, only to see if I was with another man. I wasn't that stupid to not take notice. Remember, I was a player, too.

One day one of his many women came over to confront me about him. I knew her from around and liked her. She was cool with me. I let her into the apartment and we began to talk about what kind of a dog he really was. She told me she was pregnant by him and shared the history of their rocky relationship. He walked in the door and threatened her telling her to never come back to my apartment. Later that week, he jumped on her in my building's parking lot. I heard a woman screaming loudly and desperately. I ran and opened the door to see him outside in the middle of the parking lot, kicking and punching the woman. He pulled out her hair, kicked and stomped her in the stomach, punched her in the face, and left her lying in the parking lot, bleeding and unable to move. I ran down the steps to help her, but he turned and chased me back inside. Thank God, someone called an ambulance; however, no one called the police. She recovered but lost her baby. I didn't leave the apartment for about a week. I was so scared he would do the same thing to me. I knew I had to get away from him. I wasn't about to let him hurt me. I had to live for my baby.

I called Momma and begged her to let me come home. Later that week, my baby and I moved back in with her. After a few months, he found me. He showed up at my Momma's front door. I was shocked. I couldn't believe he had found me. I told him to go away and that I was done with him. I didn't want to tell Momma because I knew she would cut him with one of her many knives. She wasn't going to stand by and let a man put his hands on her baby girl. In the end, for some strange reason, he didn't hurt me and we remained friends.

Another boyfriend, whose name I will not mention, got a little rowdy with me and Momma found out. When he came over to the house to visit, Momma invited him in and held a machete to his throat. She explained that she would hunt him down and kill him—if she heard any more about him trying to rough me up. He was so scared. He hung around but never made another attempt to get physical with me.

RaShod and I had to sleep on the couch. Luckily, it was a comfortable, large, three-piece sectional. "The Baby Elephant House" looked exactly as it did when we lived there years before. It had been painted but was still in bad shape.

At night, small mice running up and down, inside the walls, would occasionally fall on me, causing me to wake up screaming. The mouse holes were visible, so I could see their tails moving back and forth. Nonetheless, I was grateful Momma let me stay with her.

Momma had bought her first car, and had a full-time job doing what she loved: cooking. At the same time, she was taking care of RayRay and me. She bought him diapers, food, clothes and anything else he needed.

I was hanging out with my friends—drinking, smoking, and clubbing. Every Friday, Saturday, and Sunday, Momma would go to the bootlegger's house, which sold illegal whiskey on weekends. She would get so drunk that she would chase all my girlfriends out of the house with her machete. She would come in the house calling us *bitches* and *hoes.*

"Get out my house, stanky bitches." She was dating a man that she beat up every weekend. By this time in my life, I had gotten used to her violent behavior and my friends just laughed it off. It didn't bother them a bit. It didn't stop them from coming back every weekend. Momma loved me enough to take my baby and me in and provide for us both, so I was able to overlook the abuse and appreciate her help.

******

We lived at the Baby Elephant House for a few years until Momma found a new house nearby. We packed up and moved to the better house, which had two nice-sized bedrooms, kitchen, bathroom, a large screened-in porch, and a fenced backyard. This house was a big improvement. One day, Momma came home and told me she had met a new man and was moving in with him. She said I had 30 days to find a new place. She wasn't taking anybody with her. It was her time to do her own thing.

At that time I was dating a wonderful guy, so I felt like moving out would be easy. After all, I had a man. He and his family were so good to RayRay and me. We spent the weekends at his mother's home. We would have big barbecues and invite everyone over from my job and his. We went on trips and hung out. He was special to me, but I didn't take the relationship seriously. I told him Momma was moving and I had to move out. He and I talked about getting our own place. I worked and saved up my checks for two months, so I could help with the deposit and first month's rent. We looked at many apartments, found one that we could afford, and were approved very quickly. When I told him we got the apartment, he wasn't man enough to confess that he didn't want to leave his momma's house. He backed out and left me hanging with nowhere to go. He suggested that I move in with him and his momma. Momma always told me, "Never lay up with a man in his momma's house. I didn't raise you like that." I didn't feel comfortable sleeping with him in his mother's house, and besides, I had a baby. I left him and moved into my best friend's small two-bedroom apartment, which we shared with her and her baby daughter. Again, I was moving in on someone else, but I'd rather move in with my friend than lay up with a man in his momma's house without being married. He came over a few times to see me. I kicked him to the curb. What kind of man leaves his girlfriend and her baby outdoors and has the nerve to come over to somebody else's house to see her? A low-down selfish dog!

I stayed with my girlfriend for three months. Then, I found a one-bedroom apartment close by. The rent was $225 a month, water included. It was closer to my job, and if push came to shove, I could walk to work. I was tired of catching rides back and forth to work. I was 23 years old with my first place of my own. I was so happy. I vowed never to be homeless again as long as I had breath in my body. I was not going to let my children be homeless. I moved in with nothing but a bed.

My Second Baby Boy

Seven years after RaShod was born, I gave birth to another baby boy, Jahleel, 6 pounds and 3 ounces. He was an adorable baby with red curly hair and bright skin. He looked better than some girl babies. I was dating his father for a couple of years and this baby was conceived out of love. I didn't have to deliver this child alone. I had his father and grandmother right by my side. It made a difference in both my life and Jahleel's. I met Jahleel's father working in a warehouse that distributes popular snack brands across the south. When I saw this new, chocolate, thick, handsome guy walking through my department, I was eager to know his name. He was quiet and didn't waste any time noticing me. After he worked there for a few weeks, he started talking and flirting with me and made a few visits to my apartment after work. He remained a gentleman. He loved meeting RayRay, who was about two years old. He hung around for a while, until he joined the military. Somehow, we kept in contact through writing, friends, and co-workers. After he returned from the military, he showed up at my job after the shift was over to visit his brother who also worked there. The truth is that he came to see me. I was so glad to see him. He asked me out on a date and we became an item.

He was a hard-working man and had so many goals. He went to truck driving school, graduated, and obtained his commercial driving license (CDL). He found work on the road and started driving; only returning home twice a month. He was a great father figure for RayRay. He took my son many places and his family adored RaShod. He was a proud father.

Young and dumb, I was still going to the club and partying uncontrollably with no regard for him. I was hanging out in the streets with my girls while he was more serious about our relationship. As time went by, our relationship deteriorated and he became physically abusive. We had a big fight, and when I moved to a bigger apartment, he didn't move with me. We were officially broken up, but he didn't want to accept that. One night he came and picked up the boys so they could spend the night at his parents' house. Very early the next morning, I felt a blow to my head. Jahleel's father dragged me out of the bed. He was dressed in Army fatigues and was livid. I had never seen him this angry; I was literally shaking. I was terrified. He got my .380 out of the closet where I kept it hidden from RaShod. He put some bullets in the chamber and told me he was going to kill me. He forced me to call my two closest friends and tell them if they wanted to see me alive, they better come and save me. He wanted them to come over so he could shoot them as well. Thank God neither answered the phone. I begged him to tell me why he was doing this. He said that someone told him they saw me at the movies with my best male friend. I tried to explain to him that my companion was only a friend and it was nothing... he wanted to get me out of the house to enjoy a movie after being cooped up for weeks with the baby. He got angrier and started chasing me around the apartment. He started pulling my hair out, choking, and punching me. I was screaming and begging him to stop. He ripped my nightgown off and I stood naked, begging him not to shoot me, "I am your baby's momma. Please don't take his momma away from him!" Eventually, he calmed down, put the gun back in the closet, and took off in his car. I was so terrified I didn't know what to do. I had never been a victim of domestic violence. He had never hit me in all the years we dated. I couldn't tell anyone, especially Momma. I had seen Momma beat men down and I knew she would cut him, probably killing him. I couldn't tell my best friends because I was so embarrassed and ashamed. How could I tell my girls that I had to get my hair cut really short because he pulled so much out? Or that the reason I had ruptured blood vessels in my eyes was that my baby's daddy choked me? I watched the Lifetime Network and had seen movies about abuse. Now I understood domestic violence. I didn't call the police. Part of me still loved him—at least the man I first met.

After that incident, things got worse. He started leaving me death threats, which went on for awhile. I couldn't believe this was happening to me. I was tough. I vowed no man would ever hit me… and if he did that would be the last of him. I had girlfriends who were in abusive relationships and I never thought it would be me. At one point, I even believed it was my fault he had turned into this jealous monster. Prior to my becoming pregnant, there was an incident one night when he was on the road and I had a male friend over for a visit. I must admit he was quite fine, and I was both physically and sexually attracted to him. We were sitting in the living room on my green leather couch talking, laughing, and flirting. I was dressed in a skimpy nightie and drinking an alcoholic beverage. Suddenly, there was a knock on the door. It was my boyfriend. I could see him peeping through the blinds, the ones he would tell me to close because anybody could walk up, see right through them, and come in to hurt us. His warnings had backfired on me; I was busted! I couldn't believe he was standing outside knocking on the door. I jumped up and opened the door. He walked in and spoke to my male friend... he called him by his first name. To my surprise, they knew each other from high school. They spoke and eventually my friend left. I knew I was in trouble. How could I explain this? I tried to tell him some bullshit story. We got into an argument and he left. I spent the next few days begging for his forgiveness and asking him to come back. He did and we moved on but I guess the event left a lasting impression on him.

We had three ugly custody battles by the time Jahleel was five. So I became a single black woman with two baby daddies and no husband. This was not how I planned to live. This was not the future I planned for my sons. They were supposed to grow up with a father figure in their lives, not end up like my sister and me with no father around.

******

Jahleel was born with asthma and started suffering from it when he was two months old. He spent a lot of time in the emergency room and had several weeks of hospitalization. He was a champ. He always seemed so strong. He is the most competitive person I know. He is talkative and loves to debate. He loves to read any kind of book and test his knowledge on how well he knows the subject. He's basically a straight-A student... one time receiving a 99 on his CCT test. He was tested in the second grade for the Gifted Program and participated in that for a few years. He did Reading Bowl in the fourth grade; received a trophy for Rocket Reader in the fifth grade; the principal's award for making straight A's in the sixth grade; the Math trophy; and came in sixth place at the school's one-mile marathon race in the fourth grade while not allowing his asthma to stop him. As time went by, his father and I developed a decent relationship. He picks Jahleel up every Christmas and summer break. He makes sure Jahleel has everything he needs and most of the things he wants. When Jahleel graduated from the fifth grade and RaShod graduated from high school, Jahleels's father and grandmother came to both graduation ceremonies. He came to my house for the first time and it was pleasant. Today, we can hold a respectful conversation and even share a few laughs.

CRIME DOESN'T PAY:
YOU REAP WHAT YOU SOW

"Bad Girls, Bad Girls, whatcha gonna do?

Whatcha gonna do when they come for you?"

I had grown comfortable stealing all my clothes and shoes. I stole small accessories such as nail polish, makeup, jewelry, and perfume right off the counters at the major department stores, hair products, and sometimes food. When I started shoplifting in my early teen years, it was just to get the latest designer clothes and shoes so I could fit in at school. I began taking matching panty and bra sets, different colored stockings, and dress shoes. For some reason, I didn't like to wear tennis shoes. Even then I knew I wanted to be a diva. I would look at all the beautiful white models on the commercials on TV and wanted to look like them. I wanted to have long straight hair, blue eyes, and long eyelashes. I wanted to have their smooth, tanned skin. My skin was all scarred from the whippings I got as a little girl. I just wanted to feel beautiful. After all, no one had ever told me I was beautiful or smart. So, to fill that void, I started to steal.

I got away with it so many times, it became easy. I took big bags with me and would walk to local retail stores with every desire to walk out with merchandise. Around the age of 13, I decided to steal some panties and bras from my favorite store. I had shoplifted at this store for so long, it was as easy as 1-2-3. As I made it to the exit doors, a policeman was there to greet me. I sat in the back seat of the police car while listening to the officer scold me about stealing. He asked my age and telephone number, and then he called Momma. *Oh, my God! Not Momma!* I started to cry. He talked to me about the consequences of my actions and Momma told him she would make sure I would never steal again. I knew I was going to get the whopping of my life. The ride to my house was only about 15 minutes, but it was a long ride home. Of course, Momma beat my butt and dared me to put my hands on anybody else's stuff. "Yes, Ma'am. Momma, I promise. I won't steal again." A few weeks later, I was right back at it. How else was I going get new designer clothes and shoes?

About a year later, I got caught stealing again in the same store. This time I was handcuffed and put in the back seat to take a ride to juvenile detention. Momma was called off her job, and you never call an angry black woman off her job to come pick up her child from juvi. Momma came and whopped me all the way home. That didn't stop me either. I was on a roll. I was shoplifting every weekend. Me, my cousin, and some close friends started catching the bus to bigger malls, taking more and more and more. At 18, I got caught again. I was not taken to juvi but to the big house. This time I had to go to court and pay a fine. I managed to get off with a slap on the wrist. I slowed down, but I never quit. Habits are hard to break, bad habits even harder.

******

Years passed and I was 27 with two children, one 7 years old and one 7 months old. Some girlfriends and I got up one Saturday in March to go shoplifting at a local mall. We all drove in one car. In the Chinese clothing store, I packed my baby stroller with all kinds of clothing. At the door, the wife of the store owner approached me. I ran out of the store and she caught up with me. We started to tussle over the clothes, which were surrounding my baby. At this time, all my friends had run out to the car. I bit the lady's hand so she would let go of me and ran down the hall out the exit door to the parking lot. As I ran to the car, I left Jahleel behind in the middle of the parking lot in his stroller. The police had me surrounded. Again, I was handcuffed and put in the back seat of the car, my 7-year-old son standing at the car crying. After sitting in the car for a while, I went to the police station inside the mall, answered some questions, and was taken to lockup until I could see a judge on Monday morning.

The next morning I called home to see if my children were alright and to keep my friends posted on my bail. I heard all my friends in the background talking about me like a dog and laughing. I don't know why I called Momma. I didn't need her to come and get me and I didn't need any money. She cussed me out and hung up the phone. I was so hurt. After all, were they any better than me? How can the coffee pot call the tea kettle black? At that moment, I knew I had to change my ways. I knew how many friends I really had. Monday came around and I had to meet the judge at the county jail. My male friend posted bail and came to pick me up. I was so ashamed. I couldn't wait to go home to take a long, hot bath and put on some clean clothes. I had been wearing the same clothes for two days. Thank God Momma had taught us how to wash out our panties in the sink and hang them up to dry. She told us, "Always wear clean drawers. You never know if you will fall out and the ambulance has to pick you up."

This was the most trouble I had ever been in. A year later, I was convicted of third-degree robbery instead of a misdemeanor because I fought the store owner's wife and that is considered using force. I was facing a sentence of a year and one day jail time. I was thoroughly afraid of losing my children to Department of Family and Children Services (DFACS). I couldn't afford a lawyer, so was appointed one that didn't give a damn about my situation or me. I had a choice to plead guilty to felony third-degree robbery and apply for probation or risk it and go to trial. If I was found guilty, I would go to jail. My lawyer made it clear that I didn't have a chance in hell to beat the case, so I pleaded guilty and applied and was granted a year probation sentence and $800 restitution. I paid the fine, showed up once a month to see my probation officer, and it didn't take long for my year and a day to pass.

I had heard of people getting pardons for their crimes. I knew in order for me to get a good job I would need a pardon. I called my probation officer and asked her about the process. She called the Pardon and Parole Board in Montgomery, Alabama and put in a request for a pardon. I had been a good girl; I hadn't gotten in any more trouble and I had walked a straight line. I requested an application for my pardon over the phone. I filled out the lengthy application and mailed it back. A year later, I heard they received my application. They put it on file and claimed they would mail me a date soon to plead my case in front of the Pardon and Parole Board. Years went by and I didn't hear anything. Every now and then I would call to check on my status. In 2003, I called the Pardon and Parole Board and begged an officer to take another look at my case. He did and a few weeks later, I got a letter in the mail requesting that I write or appear in person to stand before the Pardon and Parole board to plead my case. I was ecstatic. Finally, after five long years of waiting, calling, and hoping, I was going to Montgomery to beg for forgiveness and another shot at life.

I called my best friend Sheila and asked her to go with me and testify on my behalf if needed. In March of 2003, I made that three hour drive to Montgomery. I was nervous but knew it was my only shot at redemption. This was going to open previously closed doors for me. I was tired of getting rejected for jobs. Employers wouldn't even give me the chance to explain what happened. I didn't actually take a gun and rob someone or break into a house or business, but this is the way it came across.

I got to Montgomery and made it to the Pardon and Parole Board. I looked around and saw all the other people sitting in there, waiting for their turn to go up in front of the six people on the board. The board contained three middle-aged white women, one black woman, one middle-aged black man, and a middle-aged white man. At last, my name was called by one of the board members. "Johnnetta McSwain? Is Johnnetta McSwain present?"

"Yes, Ma'am, I am here." I walked up to the front of the bench. I couldn't help but stare into their eyes.

"Why should we grant you a pardon today? What do you have to say for yourself?"

I only had a few minutes to plead my case. I said, *"Ladies and gentlemen of the board, I stand humbly before you today asking for your forgiveness for my crime. I am begging for a second chance today."* I went on to explain all the things I was doing—going to school, moving to Georgia, etc.

After a few minutes, I heard a voice say, *"Well done, you will be granted a pardon today."* They all commended me for turning my life around. I was so happy; I thanked them all and walked out a free woman. Sheila and I stopped at a restaurant to celebrate my newfound freedom. A few weeks later, I received a certified copy of my pardon with the seal.

Johnnetta McSwain

PART 4

THE SISTA ACT
As told by Sonya Tate

I love my sister so much. She was all I had while growing up. She protected me all the time. Sonya Tate was born February 24, 1969—11 months before me. My sister was mean, angry, and violent, just like my mother; that was the way we were raised. Sonya's problems started around the third grade, long after we moved from my grandmomma's house. The sexual abuse had pretty much ended; except for the times my uncle came to visit my mother. The trauma from the sexual and mental abuse induced severe anger and defiant behavior in Sonya and the consequences of this reaction are shared in her words on the following pages.

ACTING OUT

I became suicidal. I was angry with everybody, including God. I would pray and ask God to let me die lonely. I even made up a song: "Lord, please let me die. Lord, please let me die." I wondered why I would always sing this song, until I realized I felt angry, lonely, and depressed.

In about the seventh grade, I became extremely violent, explosive, and out of control. I got suspended from school because I threw desks and books at my teacher after someone stole the ten dollar bill Momma gave me to buy a pair of shoes. That was the only pair of shoes I was going to get for the year. When I told my teacher the money was missing, she ignored me. I started flipping over chairs and everyone ran out of the classroom screaming for Johnnetta to come and calm me down. Momma was called into a meeting and the school board decided I was mentally challenged. They put me in Special Education because they didn't know what else to do with me at that time.

No one knew about the abuse. Changing classes made things worse. I thought I must be crazy and mentally challenged if they put me in Special Education, so I acted accordingly.

I started fighting anyone that would look at me strangely. If I thought people were thinking badly about me or knew something about me, I would hit them. I remember one time I gave Johnnetta and Momma some rat poison. They don't have any memory of this. The voices in my head were telling me to kill; to get rid of all the people that hurt me. I tried the over-the-counter pills that Momma used to control her chronic asthma. I would take all her pills, get really sick, and then throw up. The voices in my head got stronger. They told me to kill myself, nobody loved me, nobody cared, and that I had no one.

I wanted to be a serial killer. I wanted to be noticed. I wanted to reveal my pain to the world. I was tired of being the only one who knew I was in pain.

******

On the way to school, we used to cross over a bridge with a major interstate below. I would stop and watch all the 18-wheelers and sometimes make hand gestures at them so they would blow their loud horns. I would also imagine jumping over the bridge and getting run over by an 18-wheeler.

I started stealing from family members and people in the church. I would rummage through their belongings to steal money and other valuables like jewelry. It became exciting to me. Nobody wanted me visiting their homes or coming around. Whenever I was confronted about stealing, I would swear I knew nothing about their missing money or valuables. I started getting angry and violent, sometimes running away for days or weeks at a time. I would call home and tell my family I was miles away and they should come and get me. Momma and Johnnetta would worry about me and walk for miles looking for me, when all the time I would be down the street at someone's house. I got beaten all the time for acting out in school, church, and home. I didn't care about getting a whooping. I started cussing Momma out and trying to fight her... but I never won.

The voices started to magnify and I became irrational. I began to fight in and out of school. I fought the biggest bully in high school. This girl was huge. She was about six feet tall, muscular, black, mean, and ugly. She pushed everyone around, including the boys. She was vicious, but she was no match for me. We began to fight and the war started. I have to admit I was scared of her. I had never been scared of anyone. I had never lost a fight. The voices told me to kill her.

I walked over to my daddy's momma's house, stole her gun, and took it to school to shoot the bully. I pulled the trigger but a classmate knocked the gun out of my hand. I was lucky a teacher didn't see the gun. I never knew what happened to that gun.

We moved and I started attending another high school. One day, this same bully came and hunted Johnnetta down while she was walking from school. The bully jumped Johnnetta, ripping the brand new dress Momma had just made her. She and her friend slapped, kicked, and stomped my sister and left her lying on the viaduct. I found out about it and walked the streets to find the bully and kill her with one of Momma's many machetes. She'd better thank God I didn't find her. Years later, I saw her and we were able to talk about what happened and forgave each other. The war was finally over between us.

In the eleventh grade, the fighting was pretty much over and I got mostly A's, but I didn't want to be around other people. I wanted to be alone. I dropped out of high school... continuing the cycle.

FINALLY, SOMEBODY TO LOVE ME

T he first time I liked a boy and had consensual sex, I got pregnant. I was 15. He went to school with me. He was the first boy I ever loved. In fact, he was the first male figure I ever loved. We didn't have sex right way. He didn't pressure or force me. This was very different from what my uncles used to do to us. When we finally had sex, I got pregnant. I was afraid to tell Momma. I had already caused her so much pain and grief. Now, I was going to create shame and embarrassment in front of the entire church and neighborhood. Momma was devastated and couldn't face me. I was very happy about having a baby. I stole $500 from a church member and bought baby strollers and other accessories. A close family friend said my baby was going to look like a monkey. I was so hurt I cried for days. Momma never spoke up for Johnnetta and me when people said ugly things about us, especially church members.

I was angry with Momma, at people in the church, at everybody. I just wanted to get away. I moved to Detroit to live with my uncle and aunt for a few months, thinking the situation would be better there.

It turned out things were just as bad in Detroit, so I called my pastor and begged her to send for me. She did and I came back home.

At six months, I gave birth to a baby girl. I named her Sharon Denise Tate after one of my best friends in the church. She was the most beautiful baby I had ever seen. She was wrapped up in one of those striped baby blankets they give you in the hospital. She had 10 little pink fingers and toes, a head full of dark curly hair, and soft skin. She smelled so good. I could tell the nurses had just given her a sponge bath and put baby lotion and powder on her. The baby lived two hours and died in my arms, but not without looking at me first. I remember those tiny little black eyes opening and staring into my eyes. I started crying when I saw her take her last breath. She was gone. The nurses came and took her away.

I couldn't afford to give her a proper funeral and burial, so the hospital buried her in a wooden box in an unmarked grave in the city cemetery. Momma and Johnnetta accompanied me at the burial. When I got home, I was so depressed. I was so angry with God for taking my baby. He knew I needed that baby. He knew that baby was the only person who would love me. This was my chance to really love someone. After Sharon Denise died, I started having nightmares. I would hear the baby crying at night, so I turned to my teddy bear for comfort.

At age 17, I started dating a young man, fell in love, and got pregnant at 18 with my second daughter. He and I were inseparable, so everybody thought. I was young and liked another guy that lived in the neighborhood. I started secretly fooling around with him. I got pregnant two months later with my third daughter, unsure of her father's identity. I was forced to tell everybody, even my boyfriend that I had been sleeping with the guy up the street. My boyfriend stepped up to the plate and asked me to marry him. I did love him but I think the main reason I married him was to move out of the house and make sure my babies had a daddy. After all, the other man had no job, little education, and no house—he lived with his momma.

We had a nice wedding. A family member owned a home about 45 minutes from Momma, so we moved there. I started sneaking the car, driving to Momma's, and disappearing up the street to see the other man. Things got bad. My husband became physically and emotionally abusive. I packed up all my belongings and left him. I moved back in with Momma until an apartment in the project was available for me. A year later, we separated.

ROCK BOTTOM

I moved out of Momma's house and into a huge project complex with a reputation of housing drug dealers and crack heads. It wasn't long before I hooked up with the man with whom I had been cheating. I moved him in with my daughters and me. Soon, he introduced me to crack cocaine. I never smoked cigarettes or weed. Occasionally, I would sip a wine cooler or similar alcohol. I thought I could handle smoking with him, but I couldn't. I started to neglect my children. I sold everything in my house: the glass table Momma had bought me, the television, the microwave, the china from my wedding, the food stamps, even the food. The children's daddy was giving me $50 per week for the girls and I spent it on crack.

I started smoking full-time. I began stealing from Momma and Johnnetta. I stole Johnnetta's expensive suede and leather suits, dresses, and jewelry. Johnnetta told me that one night she was at a popular nightclub and saw someone wearing her black suede dress. She knew I had sold it for drug money. She started to hear on the street that I was smoking crack and she and Momma asked me about

it. I got angry and violent and argued, "I am not smoking no crack."
I was in denial. My kids were hungry and I was still smoking crack.
The children were dirty. Their clothes were dirty. I didn't care.

One day my DHR worker came by to see if I was doing
right by my children. I had just gotten my food stamps and sold
all of them. I had no gas, no lights, and no food. The children were
hungry. That morning, the girls woke up and got the cereal off the
top of the refrigerator and wasted it all over the living room floor
downstairs. They had gotten cold bologna from the refrigerator and
had it all over the floor as well. I was in the bedroom naked with my
boyfriend, high all night from crack. The social worker told me to
call the children's father to pick them up. I started crying. The girls'
daddy came to pick them up, never to return them again.

By this time, my boyfriend and I had a baby boy. I didn't
send him off with my daughters. Because of the heavy drug activities,
I couldn't pay my bills. So, before I got evicted, I left the projects and
moved to a drug house with my baby boy. There were several other
children in the crack house. People would call us mothers 'Crack
Heads' and 'Geek Monsters' around the children. I felt so bad that I
would go into the bathroom to hit the pipe so nobody could see me.
I would think about my two girls and cry. This just made me want
to smoke more and more so I couldn't feel the pain of abandoning
my baby girls.

I took my baby boy to live with his daddy. I knew my girls
were protected and in a better place. I wanted the same thing for my
baby boy. I knew the monsters that were coming in and out of the
dope house where I was staying and it was not a good place for him
to be. I knew there was a chance he could get molested, raped, or
sodomized.

I went to see him only when I was clean for a few days. I
stayed so high all the time, so I didn't have to feel or think about
what was going on. I was constantly high. There wasn't a minute that

I wasn't high. Sometimes, I only ate once a week. I wasn't sleeping. I wasn't bathing. I would smoke so much crack that I would shake and twitch. I didn't want to feel the anger and the hurt. I wanted to die, just die. I was a demon. I constantly thought to myself, *I am going to hell.* I got no children, no momma, no daddy, no love. I got nobody."

I started having crack cocaine seizures. I started hearing voices again. I stopped combing my hair. It was so nappy, I had to use hair grease and lotion just to get the comb through it. The crack had turned my teeth dark gold. I didn't know what soap was anymore. I was so funky, you could smell me a mile away. I didn't know what clean panties were and stopped using deodorant and pads. When I got my period, I would stuff paper towels between my legs and keep on trickin'. I was "fiending" so bad, nothing stopped me—nothing! I slept on park benches or the ground. I ate whatever food I could find out of garbage cans. I was a nasty, stinky mess.

The first time I turned a trick, I just wanted to get high. When I got into cars, I would recite the Lord's Prayer: *"Our Father which art in heaven, Hallowed be thy name. Thy kingdom come. Thy will be done in earth, as it is in heaven. Give us this day our daily bread. And forgive us our debts, as we forgive our debtors. And lead us not into temptation, but deliver us from evil: For thine is the kingdom, and the power, and the glory, forever. Amen."* (Matthew 6:9-13, King James version). *Please, God, don't let this man kill me.* As soon as I escaped with my life, I would do it again and again. I didn't care.

I started a career in prostitution. In the 'hood, we say *trickin'.* I was jumping in and out of cars. I was sometimes getting thrown out of cars. My body was there but my mind wasn't. I was numb. I would close my eyes really tight. My mind thought it was not happening to me. There were no emotions, no feelings, no movements; nothing. I would think to myself, *Oh, what the hell? It will be over in a minute.* Then, I would go back and smoke. I got to the point where I just needed the money. I would have threesomes with women and men, give blow jobs, and whatever it took to get high.

I had a sting gun I used to rob people. I would break into people's houses and steal their appliances. I would knock on people's doors, tie them up, rob them, and then run down alleys to escape. I would sell the stolen goods for crack. I stole people's checks out of their mailboxes, forged their names, and cashed them. That lifestyle continued for over 10 years.

Just One More

I had been up for four or five days. Late one night, I decided to go on the beat to turn a trick to get more drugs. I was walking up and down the beat, a popular street known for crack heads strolling and looking for johns. A red SUV and a blue Lexus were racing up and down the street. I stopped to watch them, hoping they would want a blow job or sex so I could get a rock. It worked; one of the cars stopped and picked me up. I was so high I could barely walk, but the drugs were calling me—just one more, just one more… my gut feeling told me the men were up to no good, but the drugs took over.

I was really nervous about getting in the truck—something told me not to but I did anyway. I said, "Hello, I'm Sonya. Let's go somewhere more secluded." We parked by some railroad tracks where there were bushes and trees. This helped conceal our identity from the police. I was known by every police officer working my beat. I had already been to jail for improper soliciting. A quiet voice said to me, *you need to move.* I convinced him this was not a good place. There were no lights, no passing cars, nothing but pure darkness. So he moved the truck and parked near a small blue house on the street.

Before I knew it, the SUV he had been racing pulled up behind us. A young man got out, and at that very moment, I knew I had to jump out of that truck. He walked up with a silver .22. He said, "Bitch, you gonna give it up."

I said, "No, brother, don't do me like this, I'm your sista. It ain't like that. Please don't hurt me."

He started shooting at me, unloading his gun. Mercifully, all the bullets missed me; the gunpowder from one of the bullets hit my baby finger. I screamed, "Man, you shot me! You shot me!" I started running for my life. I ran to a house and started to beat on the door. Nobody answered. He ran back to his truck and pulled off. Once again, my life was spared. That Lord's Prayer must have worked. I ran back to the dope house and shared my experience with my friends.

I quickly got over it and changed my clothes to return back to the same street to do the exact same thing, so I could get my high back. My friends warned me not to go back, but I did anyway. I didn't need to but wanted to. *Just one more rock, just one more rock and I'll call it a night.* Ten minutes later, I was back on the beat. By this time, I had turned a successful trick and gotten an eight ball. Suddenly, I saw a man running toward me. He didn't look familiar, and it was so dark I couldn't really see his face. I stopped to see why he was running, and as he got closer, I saw that same silver gun. He yelled, "Bitch, you should've given it up!"

I started to run, but there was nowhere to go. The night was pitch-black, no streetlights, no cars riding by, no shield, and no protection. He started shooting at me. I felt a bullet hit my leg. I ran to a different house, opened the screen, and fell into the door. He stood over me and shot me four times, point blank into my legs, while laughing and saying, "I told you, Bitch, you should've gave it up."

I threw my hands in the air and said, "Lord, I ain't ready to die." The ambulance came and took me to the hospital. It made the morning news. My mother was called at her job at about 5 a.m. and was told, "Your daughter has been shot."

A church member had called my sister and said, "I saw your sister on the news. She's been shot."

By the time my mother got to the hospital, I wanted to die. I didn't want her there. She had never been there for me. *Why is she here now? What does she care?* I asked God to take my life. I no longer needed to live in this pain. I had four holes the size of a penny in my legs. I only weighed 80 pounds, so the bullets went straight through my legs. You could see straight through the holes. I remember the doctors cleaning the cavities with long Q-tips.

Two weeks later, I was riding a ten-speed to get more crack. The wounds were bleeding but I didn't care. All I wanted to do was get high.

Enough Is Enough

I remember walking by a mirror and glancing at my body frame. I was in shock when I saw my thin, frail, 80-pound body. Crying uncontrollably, I walked to the cemetery and sat on a tombstone in the rain. I prayed to God and asked him to have mercy on my soul. "Please, send me somewhere I can get help."

A few days later, I hooked up with my regular "John" and got some crack. I was on my way home when the police passed by me. I heard a voice say, "Get rid of your crack and your stem." I threw it all in the bushes. They came back around and took me to jail for loitering. I had no identification on me. I was angry that they took me to jail, and I didn't understand why until later. It was then that I remembered that I had prayed to God to get me some help. This was the answer to my prayers, though I didn't listen at the time. I did three months in the city jail. I got out and continued the same path—stealing, robbing, smoking, and trickin'.

About six months later, I got arrested for prostitution but did no time. I received one year of probation. As soon as I hit my 12th

month of probation, I was in a crack house getting high again. The police busted the house and took me to jail. I served six months for prostitution and paraphernalia.

While I was in jail, my daughters' daddy brought them to visit me. I was so hurt for my girls to see me in jail. I made myself a promise at that time: I would never go back to jail; nevertheless, when I got out, I went right back to the streets. This time, I had learned not to take all my money to the dope man. I realized I needed to eat, so that I could gain weight... *and I did!* I was living in a trailer with no water. I urinated in a bucket. I had to go outside and get water out of a hydrant to bathe. Early one cold morning, the trailer burned to the ground from a defective plug on a small electric heater I was using to keep warm.

I lost everything I had. I moved into a shelter and stayed clean long enough to get a job. I was still doing drugs on the low-low. In 2003, I started seeing a psychiatrist because of the suicidal thoughts, depression, and anger. I was having seizures. I was diagnosed with paranoid schizophrenia and major depression. I was taking 12 different kinds of medications at night. Strangely, I started feeling better. I attended group therapy, individual therapy, and anger management. I learned how to journal. This helped me so much. Someone talking to me and showing me love really helped me heal. I got another job at a popular restaurant. Momma invited me to church and I went and re-joined the church. I had a relapse a couple of times but I didn't quit. I didn't give up. I had a supportive pastor and co-pastor praying and pulling for me to overcome this disease.

*****

In 2007, I married a man I had been dating off and on for a few years. We once did drugs together but are now both clean. I have been living in my own place for three years drug free. God has blessed me with new furniture, a new mind, and a new will to live. In 2008, I was diagnosed with HIV. I don't know where or when I contracted it. I could have gotten it from anybody. I take full responsibility. I jumped in so many cars, turned tricks with so many men—some in the same night, most of whom didn't use condoms. The doctors have been testing me constantly to make sure their diagnosis is accurate. But, I know there is a God that has the last word.

Today, Sonya is an advocate for HIV education. She is truthfully speaking at churches, schools, and community centers. She is an active member in church. She is currently studying for her GED and hopes to obtain her Associates degree in Substance Abuse Counseling. She wants to major in Social Work. The making of the documentary and the 12 steps created by her sister have inspired her to strive to be a better person, to love herself, to stay clean. She has become closer to her mother and sister. Unfortunately, she is still battling crack cocaine and depression.

PART 5

The Decision

Unhealthy Relationship:
Love Gone Bad

After the birth of RaShod, I gave up on love. I had loved Henry so hard and for so long, I was a bitter woman with lots of baggage. I swore I would be a playa for life. I would dog every man that came in my path… I would lie, I would cheat, and I would only want his money and the material things he could give me. I didn't have time for love. Tina Turner had just come out with "What's Love Got to Do with It," which became my motto. I knew all the lyrics, and my favorite part of the song was, "What's love got to do… got to do with it? Who needs a heart when a heart can be broken?"

However, there was one man that got my attention. I was 27 and he was 40. My girlfriend was dating a man with a loud-mouthed, flashy, single friend. She told me all about him and set it up for us to meet at a local club. I got a baby-sitter and we all rode together to meet this man. I walked into the club and went to our reserved table, which was fully dressed with bottles of champagne. I introduced myself, shook his hand, and took a seat right next to him. He was speechless. I was stunning in my shiny, patent leather, two-piece leopard print skin-tight suit. I was fine! I instantly liked him. He was loud, alley, and liked to spend money… we definitely had a lot in common. He was short, had a process, and a big round belly. He was wearing a pair of tight red leather pants like Eddie Murphy, a fur jacket with a matching hat, and his name in diamonds around his fat, short neck. He asked to take me home to see where I lived. On the way home, he explained how he used to be a pimp and told me he was a thoroughbred player. He never had only one woman in his entire life, and he could not be changed. *Cha Ching!* I was in love. I loved a man who was honest and straight-up with me. At least, I knew where he was coming from and could decide if I wanted to deal with him or not.

To my surprise, we got along wonderfully. He swept me off of my feet. He paid my bills, took me on fabulous trips, and brought my boys places. He bought them all their clothes and shoes and made sure I had groceries and enough spending money to have my hair and nails done weekly. He was a lot of things to me. He was my sweet thing. He was a father figure to my boys (despite his previous lifestyle). He was a friend that supported anything I did. He was the first man who taught me how to open up a banking account and save money. He really had himself together. He was a successful, licensed barber by trade. He had gone to barber school, graduated, sat for his license, and passed the test. He owned a nice house, drove a beautiful Lexus, and wore really fly clothes and jewelry. He was so humble and helped anyone he could. Every fall, he gave free haircuts to little boys in the community to get them ready for school. Nevertheless, he was whorish and I knew he wasn't the man I was going to marry.

We had our bad times but the good outweighed the bad. As the years went by, I busted him a few times with other women. I was a little hurt but knew this was part of his lifestyle and I had accepted that.

Once he came by my apartment unannounced. He was sitting outside in his car. I came out to check on a neighbor, and as I knocked on her door, he jumped out of his car and chased me back into my apartment. He was so angry I could see the veins popping out of his face and neck. I ran into the bedroom and he gave chase. He punched me in my chest a couple of times. I was screaming and yelling. I finally convinced him there was not another man in the apartment. He left and for the first time in my life—I dialed 911. The police came and I made a police report. A few weeks later, we made up and I went back to him.

As I started to mature, I began to realize I had to make some life changes. I should have left him as soon as he hit me but I didn't. I stayed for the wrong reasons. I didn't want to give up the lavish trips, the money, the fun, and the loving. But most of all, I didn't want to disappoint my boys by taking another father figure away from them. They loved and admired him. I never told them about the fights; I wanted to protect them. Eventually, we separated but remained close friends with benefits. This was the first relationship I ever had where I learned so much about maturing and setting goals and dreams.

THE UGLY TRUTH:
A LOOK IN THE MIRROR

Happy birthday to me, happy birthday to me..." It was January 31, 2000, my 30th birthday. That day I woke up and realized I had absolutely nothing to celebrate—no money, no full-time job, no home, no husband, and no clue, not even the will to do better. As I looked around the old, yellow, raggedy Section 8 house I had been living in for about three years, I could see small roaches crawling up and down through tiny cracks in the hollow walls. I thought about the mousetraps I had secretly hidden throughout the small two-bedroom, one-bath house to catch the busy mice migrating in cracks and crevices. No matter how much money I spent on exterminators, I couldn't get rid of the generations of bugs and rodents that had occupied the house many years before I moved in. I could also see layers of different-colored paint throughout the house. I heard endless cars going by on the busy street as if I lived on a highway and the loud whistling of trains using the tracks behind the house. The train track was so close to the house I could literally read the cargos.

Some of the children in the neighborhood tried to jump on the train. At last, I knew it was time to make some changes.

I sat on the side of my black and green lacquer bed with the mirrored headboard, which I had bought about six years before for $499 from the furniture store everybody patronized when they got their income tax refunds. In addition to the bedroom suite, my girlfriends and I had bought the same three-piece glass black table set with the gold horns, oversized pictures of big cats, and new living room furniture every other year with our refunds. To complete the rooms, we all sold home interior decorations and accessories, so my rooms were filled with pictures, artificial flowers, sconces, votives, matching candles, plaques, and beautiful wall decorations. Half of Birmingham had the same furniture and accessories; however, if you didn't have any of these items, you were considered country as hell.

I began to take a good look at myself in the mirror on my matching black and green lacquer dresser. I began to see the ugly, gut-busting, nasty, low-down, dirty, tired, and unworthy Johnnetta. I saw the neglectful mother; the housing tenant; the trick; the temp; the high-school dropout; the shoplifter; the wanna-be-diva; the baby momma; the clubber; the bitch; the ho; the player; the back-stabbing, two-faced friend; the drama queen. At last, I saw the true, raw me: the woman with nothing, the woman who had no reason to be called a woman, let alone a mother.

I thought about my two boys as they lay asleep in their bunk beds. Didn't they deserve better? Didn't they deserve to grow up in a better neighborhood? Didn't they deserve a better house, with a better momma? I began to think about how every male in my family had sexually molested or touched me inappropriately at some time in my life. At this time, two of the three uncles that molested me were still living. Suddenly, I was afraid for my boys. *Oh my God, I've got to do something to save my boys.* Could this be hereditary? Could they grow up and molest their children, their friends' children, or neighborhood children? What if they became rapists, thugs, or killers? What if they turned out to be just like *all* the men in my family, either dead or in jail? The pain was so overwhelming, I cried out loud, hard, and long. I cried until my nose ran, my head pounded, and my eyes turned bloodshot red and puffy. I was exhausted. I couldn't cry anymore. I dried my face. I knew at that moment, I had to save my boys as well as myself.

As I continued to look in the mirror, I began to think about all the women in my family. My momma was a chronic alcoholic; my sister, addicted to crack cocaine; my aunt, a dope fiend; and my other aunt brutally murdered. Did I want to continue this deadly cycle?

At that moment, I thought about ways I could change the future for my family. After looking at all my downfalls, I began to think about my survival skills. I had dropped out of high school to work. I moved out of my momma's house at age 23 never to return. I had managed to keep a temporary job to take care of myself when I didn't have a sugar daddy. I had walked away from an abusive relationship to be a single parent. I had done a decent job raising my boys. I was a soccer mom, went to school programs, participated in sports events, and made sure they had a hot meal every night. I managed to provide them with name-brand clothes and shoes and nearly everything they ever asked for. I knew how to talk a good game. I could talk myself in and out of anything. I knew how to survive in the hardest of the streets. I wasn't afraid of too much of anything. But had I really been a good momma or was I only doing what I was taught?

Then and only then, I realized that what I didn't have was an education. I only had a GED, and I knew that wasn't enough. I imagined how phenomenal I would be if I had the best of both worlds: A beautiful, strong woman with street smarts, survival skills, entrepreneurial skills, intellectual skills, and an education. This would be a chance for my boys to grow up in a positive, educational environment and see their mom accomplish things they would not normally be exposed to. I knew right then that I had to get my degree. Not just my bachelor's, not just my master's, but also my doctorate. I was going to be the first in my family to obtain all three degrees. Without knowing a lot about college and what it takes to attend, I had made up my mind.

I was going to need the next 10 years to obtain this dream. First, I had to change my environment. I called all my men and told them I was done. I called my girls and told them I was moving and that I no longer wanted to hang in the streets. I sat my boys down and explained that we were poor, that we didn't have anything. I hadn't been the best momma and I promised I was going to make it up to them. I said, "We are moving to Atlanta."

The oldest asked, "When did we get poor?"

"We have always been poor. But, things are going to change. We are moving to a nicer neighborhood, better schools, better roads, and a better environment. I will start college, and I will need you to help me out with your little brother."

I wanted to get the entire college experience. I decided I was going to go to college full-time—no breaks, no job, no excuses. I had worked many temporary jobs for more than 10 years and had nothing to show for it. I was still on Section 8. I was receiving food stamps off and on whenever my assignments ended. Basically, I was still struggling. So, I said to myself, *if I can struggle all these years, surely I can struggle and make it through school. What do I have to lose?* Failure was not an option this time.

SICK AND TIRED OF BEING SICK AND TIRED

R ight after this revelation, I went to visit a friend, Veronica
Thompson, and told her of my plans to reach for my dreams.
Veronica was one of my best friends and Sheila's youngest and only
sister. Sheila had already relocated to Georgia for the same reasons I
was moving. Veronica and I had become very close and spent a lot
of time together. She was always so funny. She was the first person I
told about my dream—how I would move to Georgia, start college,
and get my first real job with benefits. I shared with her how I had
to get out of this cruel, infectious ghetto. Veronica lived in a very
drug-infested neighborhood. Thugs stood on her corner, watching
and waiting for their prey. She was a single woman with four children, and while she was at work, the thugs would break into her
small house and steal everything she had of value. This happened to
her several times. Somehow, she always managed to get back everything she lost. Veronica was my girl. I loved her so much. She always
listened to me and encouraged me no matter what anyone said. She
was always the mediator when the rest of us got into a brawl.

Around December 2001, coming up to the New Year, I put my plans into action. I called my Section 8 worker and asked for a transfer to Georgia, only to find out I did not qualify to relocate because I didn't have a voucher for another state. I could only move throughout Alabama. I would have to wait a year to move after I received my voucher. Finally, after a yearlong wait, I called my land-lord and informed her of my plans to move in 90 days. It was 2003, New Year's Day. Boxes were everywhere. People would visit and were shocked to see I had packed up my small house by myself within a matter of days, getting the strength from the adrenaline and excite-ment of a new life. I threw away everything that reminded me of my life of poverty and oppression in that house. I told Veronica I was going to Jackie Chan (Kung Fu Kick) most of my furniture outside on the curb in front of my house because I was starting over and didn't want to take the old into the new. Most of my friends thought I was joking. Some said I would never make it and that I would crawl back. Some asked, *"Why do you want to move to Atlanta? It's too much traffic."* But, it didn't matter what anyone thought or said. I was leaving them behind.

Sheila had sent me a huge apartment guide and Tracy gave me information about relocating to Cobb County. She sent the number of the gated apartment complex where she lived in Marietta. In January 2003, I drove to Atlanta with four bald tires and hardly any gas. I had to go, because I couldn't miss my appointment at the Housing Authority to sign my new voucher for housing. While I was in Georgia, I looked at Tracy's apartment complex. I was in awe. I had never seen nor heard of a gated community. As I went through the gate, I was so impressed. I immediately felt a sense of safety. I looked at the well-manicured lawn; lots of tall, beautiful, green trees waving back and forth from the cool breeze; the stream of water flowing throughout the trail around the huge complex.

I saw little children running around as I reached the rental office. The complex featured a library and a swimming pool. It offered many extracurricular activities for kids of all ages. The small children had "Kids Club" once per week after school. They would read books and watch movies. The middle-school kids and the teenaged kids each had their own group. The teenaged kids would go on exciting field trips that I could never afford for my boys. RaShod once went on an out-of-state camping trip paid for through a scholarship. They provided programs, such as *Single Mother's Night Out*, which was a way to help single mothers feel special. We would go to the movies, dinner, and what not. The apartment complex paid for it and provided free baby-sitting. Lastly, they would have family events. One time we went to Stone Mountain and had a picnic, which was the first time I had ever had a family picnic. It was beautiful. After viewing the freshly painted three-bedroom apartment on the top level with a balcony, I was completely sold. I signed my paperwork and returned to Birmingham to finish packing. My move-in date was March 7, 2003. I was so excited that during the whole drive back to Birmingham, I didn't even think about the possibility of one or more of my tires bursting on the highway.

THE MOVE

I reserved the largest moving truck I could afford. The man I had dated for the previous five years paid for all my moving expenses as a gift. He also had one of his maintenance men help me pack the truck, drive to Georgia, and unpack the truck. He, RaShod, and I spent long hours loading the truck. I didn't know I had so much. There wasn't enough room for everything. We would have to make a second trip. Finally, it was time to load up what we could, and then take off to I-20 east.

It was a cool, drizzling day in March. We made it to Georgia in about two hours. We pulled into the gated community and drove around to my new apartment. My helper parked the truck and we moved furniture and housewares up the two flights of stairs. Darkness had fallen and we had to hurriedly return home to make a second trip. The young man was tired and stated he wasn't able to help with the second load. I was on my own. Veronica and her husband came by to see how everything was going. I told them I had to finish loading the truck because I had to return it the next day or I would be paying huge fees. Veronica and her husband helped me and RaShod finish packing the truck to full capacity.

Now, I had to find someone to drive the truck to Atlanta. Surely, I couldn't do it. I had never driven anything bigger than my Mustang. I was afraid to drive a truck that size. But there was no turning back. I had come too far to stop. I jumped in the truck. RaShod, then 12 years old, hopped in on the passenger side. I put my foot on the gas and pulled off. I will never forget how scared I was driving that truck. Every time the wind blew, the truck swayed back and forth on the highway.

Finally, we arrived at the complex. We made it through the dark, cool, falling misty rain. With sore muscles, burning sleepy eyes, and aching backs, we worked until the wee hours of the morning moving boxes up the steps. We couldn't believe it. At last, we had moved everything into the apartment. We were too exhausted to celebrate. We lay down on the floor just to shut our eyes and regain strength for a couple of hours, because I had to return the truck by 7 a.m. to avoid late fees. The entire time I was driving to and from Georgia, I felt relief and sadness at the same time. I was leaving a life of poverty, shame, bad relationships, dead-end jobs, drinking and partying, fussing and cussing, enemies and close friends, and family. But, I was embarking on a new journey, a safer place for my children to grow up, better schools, more opportunities, a chance to start over. I wasn't sure of what was in front of me, but I knew it had to be better than what was behind me. I was so excited about my new move, I cried all night.

PART 6

New Beginnings

HOTLANTA

Settling into my roomy new apartment took some time. I had only been to the complex twice to visit Tracy when she lived there, so I didn't know my way around. The rental office was helpful and explained how to get to various places. I was drawing unemployment from my last temp job in Birmingham, thanks to my boss who had encouraged me to leave Alabama and reach for my dreams. I decided to look for another temp job until I straightened out my college admission, so I went to a few temp agencies and landed a job immediately.

I had only been in Georgia for about a week when I met Tonya Morrison at a popular business center. She was sitting at a computer next to me trying to e-mail her resume to an employer for a temp position. I looked over at her computer screen and realized we were sending our resumes to the same employer for the same position.

I said, "Are you sending your resume to the same company I'm sending mine?"

She said, "Yeah," and we both started to laugh.

What a coincidence, to be applying for the same job, at the same company, at the same time.

After we e-mailed our resumes, Tonya suggested we get lunch together at a nearby restaurant. As we ate, Tonya, then 37, told me she had just relocated to Marietta from Miami, Florida to get a fresh start. She is one of those thick, big-booty, dark-skinned girls from Miami. She arrived earlier in the year to find an apartment and a college to attend to pursue her dream of becoming a nurse. She told me she had been to Kennesaw State University to check out their nursing program. This was the very first time I had ever heard of Kennesaw State. Tonya had a nice little cozy pad around the corner from the restaurant. She had definitely done her homework. She had saved her money, paid all her bills, and paid off her little red car. Her two children stayed in Miami with her momma to finish high school. Tonya had this thick, hardcore exterior, but once you got to know her she wasn't that bad. She had a no-nonsense attitude. I had never met a woman who wasn't caught up in name-brand clothes or shoes. She was a saver and lived by a carefully structured monthly budget. She sent her children money every month and paid all her bills in full and on time. I was so impressed with her. I had never paid all my bills on time or in full, nor had I ever written a monthly budget.

We soon learned we had both gotten the job, and started right away. Unfortunately, I didn't stay long. The temporary agency called me to explain that my assignment had ended after about two weeks on the job. They said I had caused a riot because during a staff meeting I asked the supervisor how much more money the temps would receive after being hired as full-timers. I was getting paid $12 per hour as a temp. The supervisor said as full-timers we would begin making about $10 per hour.

I said, "What? We're making $12 an hour already!" At that moment, many temps got angry, grabbed their purses, and walked out. The other temps went to lunch and didn't return. I called a few other temp agencies and got another job immediately.

As I walked into the second company with my new assignment, I greeted the receptionist with my name, position, and a handshake. To my surprise, I noticed she had a catalog on her desk that read: Kennesaw State University. How coincidental was that? I remembered Tonya talking about this university. "Is that a college?"

The receptionist replied, "Yeah, this is where I go to school."

I told her I wanted to go to college, but didn't know how or where to start. She began to tell me all about Kennesaw. She told me about financial aid, Pell grants, classes, and degree programs. I was shocked!

"You mean I can go to school without having any money?" This was unbelievable!

She said, "I'm going to Kennesaw on my lunch break. If you like, you can ride with me." I met up with her on our lunch break for my first look at Kennesaw State and a whole new life.

SETTLED DOWN

"*Lights, Camera, Action, Sorry Miss Jackson*" was the song playing in the small, tightly-packed, hole-in-the-wall club. That's where I met Willie Clay.

I was sitting at the bar with Tracy, engaged in conversation with a few guys buying us drinks. Tracy said, "There's a guy over there staring at you!"

I looked through the crowd and saw him. His eyes met mine. Then, he started walking toward me. He was a cutie pie. He had a light, caramel skin complexion, a big head, and squirmy little eyes. He had his hair corn rolled (braided) to the back, and had a buff body. He stopped walking when he got to me and said, "Hey, my name is Willie." I smiled girlishly, but still I acted uninterested in anything he had to say. I finally told him my name. I was very surprised he didn't have a played-out rap or tired pick-up line.

He said, *"I think you're beautiful and I'm going to marry you."*

I was so numb to a decent man approaching me that I got angry and verbally abusive with him. I cussed him out with a few of my favorite names for men, "buster, punk-ass, good-for-nothing, rooty-pooty scrub." He told me he had been at his job for seven years and that he had his own place. He wrote his home, cell, and work numbers on a piece of paper and handed it to me.

I have to admit, I hadn't met a plain, decent man in years, especially in the places where I hung out. I wasn't used to a man approaching me in a respectful manner. I was accustomed to men saying, "Hey, Boo, when you gon' holla at yo boy?" Or something like, "I got 5 on it," or "that's a big ass, and I want to hit that!" Or the most famous line of all, "I know as good as you look, you got to have a man... but I've been watching you all night."

Before Willie, I only liked roughnecks, "ballers," hustlers, and players. A man had to step to me with plenty of game and it had to be tight or I would tell him to *GET TO STEPPING!* I was impressed that Willie had a job and his own place. I was even more impressed when he gave me all three of his contact numbers; it had been years since I met a man who actually gave me his home number. I gave him my number but played it off like I wasn't interested. He bought me a few drinks, hung around a little while longer, and walked off. I continued to talk to other dudes for the rest of the night.

About a week later, Willie called me and we talked for hours about goals, family, upbringing, love, and everything in between. I wasn't looking for a man because I was still trying to work on myself. He was too quiet; I was too loud. He was too plain; I was too jazzy. He was too relaxed; I was too energized. He was a man of few words; I was a woman of too many. I was used to aggressive men taking control and he was very reserved. I hated that. I didn't like him—he wasn't my type. He didn't have a fancy car or a truck with rims; he didn't make a lot of money or have what I thought was a good job; and he didn't wear baller clothes (*Gucci, Rocawear & Sean John*), diamond rings, furs, or necklaces. He was just too plain for me. But, opposites attract. He called me one night and asked me out on our first date—a movie and dinner of hot wings. I went to the movies and we had a pretty good time. He started calling to see if I wanted company at my place or would prefer to visit him, but I wasn't going to couch sit. I had done that at 16 and wasn't looking for a boyfriend or a husband… I wasn't looking for love at all. I had just left a long relationship and definitely did not want to start another.

I didn't want to waste his time or mine, so I told him all about my past, the sexual abuse, the games I played, and the reason I moved to Georgia. I shared with him my plans to go to college, to be the first in my family to earn all three degrees, and be a role model for my sons. I asked him about his plan and five-year goals. He said he didn't have to share that information with me. I politely told him it was nice meeting him and hung up the phone. He called back a few days later and we talked about his goals.

Surprisingly, we started hanging out often. Finally, I invited my girlfriends over to meet him and get their opinion. I knew my girls would drill him about his life and warn him about what he needed to do in order to be with me.

Willie asked me to marry him three times. The most beautiful part of his marriage proposals was when he asked my boys and me to move in with him. This is how a real man is supposed to ask a woman to marry him. Each time I said, "I don't think you're ready for me." I wrote a list of things I needed for him to do and told him to call me back once he read it over to let me know if he was really ready to be with me.

Some of the items were:

Be a man.

Pay the bills.

Take out the garbage.

Take care of the boys.

Treat me like a queen.

Handle your business.

He read the list and called me back, saying, "I'm ready." I answered, "Are you ready to take a woman and two children? Are you ready for this journey I'm about to go on? Are you ready to struggle, sacrifice, and do without?" I explained to him I was going to school for a number of years and I wasn't going to work. I had worked dead-end jobs all my life and hadn't gotten anywhere. I was going to do something different and devote 100% of my time to school. I had enough of long, tiring relationships. I finally knew what I wanted. I knew who I was and what I would and would not accept from a man or from anyone for that matter. I set boundaries on how I was going to be treated, respected, handled, talked to, and sexed. It sounded good at the time and we finally agreed we were both ready.

I chose to marry Willie because he's a hard-working man who accepted me and my past. He wouldn't give up or take no for an answer. He knew what he wanted in a woman and he wasn't afraid to go after it. He showed strength and maturity, and I admired his tenacity. I knew he was for me. He allows me to be a complete woman, not a better half. He knew I would never go for that societal label. He didn't have a problem with me being loud and crazy, hanging out with my girls, wearing whatever I want to wear, or going wherever I want to go. He has no insecurities and is filled with confidence. In fact, he thinks he's so fine and all the ladies love him. I love a man who loves himself; this means he can love me. With Willie, I never have to pretend I am something I am not.

Willie adores my two sons and has always worked on being their friend, not just their step-dad. In turn, they love him. Once I asked them both how they felt about Willie and they said, "We love him because he never has anything to say." I laugh every time I think of that. None of them have a lot to say. Nobody raises hell in our house but me. Willie is good to the boys and makes sure they have what they need. He will give them his last. He constantly shows them how a man is supposed to take care of his family.

We set a wedding date for a year and a half later. Willie worked two jobs for the next year just to pay for the ring and the wedding. We were married in Jamaica on August 4, 2004. It was beautiful, and my two best friends, Sheila and Tracy, were there right beside me to share my day.

It's been a challenge for both of us. I had to learn how to be a wife. I had to learn how to genuinely love a man, how to treat a man, how to let a man be the man of the house, how to take direction and leadership from a man, and how to shut my big mouth up. I still haven't learned how to be SUBMISSIVE. Willie supported my dreams to attend college, but things got a little rocky during the school years. He doesn't talk about my educational success to me, but he makes sure I study hard and don't fail in school. He's proud of me. Pride and love gush out of his heart. Our marriage has been peppered with ups and downs, sacrifices and compromises, and is a work in progress.

COLLEGE:
SCARED TO DEATH

We pulled up in front of this vast, attractive, well-manicured campus filled with students walking, talking, laughing, and congregating. It was a culture shock for me. I had never seen anything as striking as that before. The freshly cut green grass, the statues and artwork around the campus, the large dormitories, the many buildings displaying names and numbers that corresponded to the catalogue—it was all overwhelming. There were fliers posted all around the campus along with invitations to parties, fraternities, and campus events. Kennesaw State University is the third largest university in Georgia and has a predominately white student body with a small ratio of African-American students. I saw long lines in the bookstore, financial aid, and registrar's offices. I had never in my life been around that many white people at one time. I went to school with black people. I was sold. I knew this would be a good environment for me. I definitely wasn't going to be hanging out with all those young children. I needed to be somewhere where I couldn't drop it like it's hot. I had to be in a place where I wouldn't get in trouble, hang out with the wrong crowd, drink, steal, party, or act like a fool.

As I entered the admissions building with the receptionist from work, I didn't know what to do. I walked up to one of the student workers and said, "I need help. I want to go to college. Can you please help me?" The student so kindly held my hand and walked me through the entire process.

First, I completed the admissions application, then financial aid, and lastly, met with advisors. I filled out the paper application and turned it in to the student. I went home and electronically filled out my FAFSA. I called the community school I had attended 10 years earlier and asked them to mail my transcripts to Kennesaw State and I also got them to mail me a copy for my records. At last I called Montgomery, Alabama to ask them to mail my GED test scores to KSU and myself. After KSU received all my completed paperwork, I received a letter explaining that because I was a nontraditional student, meaning over the age of 25, I had to take a placement test to see what classes I required. Finally, after a few months, I was accepted to Kennesaw State University for spring semester, January 2003. Throughout the entire process, I was treated like a queen. I always give the Admissions Department so much credit for making a lasting effect on me. I think the way I was treated played a significant decision on my attending KSU. I never even looked at another school. The first thing I did was go to *Wal-Mart* to buy a rolling book bag; I wanted to look and feel like a student.

January 2003, spring semester, I began my first day of school as a proud, nontraditional, 33-year-old freshman. I lined up in the bookstore to buy my books. I was so excited to be a student and felt honored to be there. While in the bookstore, I saw a beautiful black cap and gown hanging there and asked if I could try them on. I wore the gown over my clothes, and then added the cap. I repeated this process at the beginning of every semester, imagining myself marching across the stage wearing that cap and gown, receiving my degree.

I felt intimidated in class. I had never seen students so damn smart. Where did they come from? I knew I wasn't smart. I couldn't ever remember making an "A" in school, ever, ever, ever. I am so glad Kennesaw had me take the placement test to determine where I needed to start. I didn't do so well on my math section, so had to begin by taking Math 97 and 98 before I could even start regular math to become a physical therapist. I had decided to major in Health, Science and Physical Education because I was already a massage therapist.

Pell grants and loans helped maintain my living expenses and allowed me to attend school full-time, taking six classes totaling 18 hours each semester. This was a bit too much, but I was dedicated, motivated, and focused. Failure was not an option. I was going to make my boys proud of me. I was going to graduate. One day during my first semester, I was sitting outside the cafeteria when one of my classmates walked up and sat with me. She brought several of her friends. Before I knew it, we were meeting there every day. We became buddies. One particular student I became close with besides Tonya was Janice Watkins. Janice was a cute, petite, feisty sista with a small frame, a little plump booty and a rich caramel complexion. She walked around that big-ass campus in her stilettos and didn't think twice about what anybody thought of her. She had a snappy attitude and would put you in your place real fast. I admired her tenacity. She had been on her own since a very young age. She moved to Georgia by herself and wasn't afraid of going anywhere alone. She would give you anything she had. She was another person that wore a tough exterior over a soft heart of gold. She was majoring in Psychology and had been in college off and on for a few years. She knew the ropes. She had two jobs and was a hard worker. She never asked anybody for anything. She had no problem with the word I-N-D-E-P-E-N-

D-E-N-T. She worked as a beauty consultant for a major cosmetics line in an upscale mall. Her makeup was flawless every day at school.

One day, she came into the Student Center, our favorite place to meet, and handed me some makeup samples—lip gloss, foundation, and pencils. She said, "Here are some colors I want you to try." She knew that my silver and gold 99¢ lipstick, black lip liner, and gold and silver eye shadow was way out of style. I was so grateful for her advice. I took some professional tips from her and immediately began applying her tips to my face. After awhile, we had many young women sitting at that table to hear me talk a little trash but mainly to listen to me speak about women having self-esteem and self-worth. I became a favorite to the students. Thank God for Janice. Today, she is one of my best girlfriends. She supports my dreams, both emotionally and financially.

BACK TO THE BASICS:
READING, WRITING, AND MATH

Adjusting to school wasn't easy; I had to start all over again. Taking at least six classes each semester was a full-time job, so I had to learn the best way to study. I had to learn how to take notes. I had to learn how to listen. Math was my hardest obstacle to overcome. I hated math with every fiber of my essence. I didn't understand why I needed to know calculus to get a job. I sat in the very front row of my Elementary Math 97 class, which was the class for beginners. I had to make sure I was on time and ready to learn. I wasn't going to let this beat me. I told myself I could pass the class; I was just as good as anyone else.

I remember sitting across from a student from Bolivia. She was so smart. She would write all the notes and come back to class the next day with every single problem completed correctly. *So, I thought to myself, in order for me to make A's, I need to study with her.* So I did. I asked if I could study with her and she agreed to it.

She wasn't proficient in English, so asked if we could make a trade-off—I would help her in her English classes and she would help me in math; worked for me. She wouldn't give up on me. She would stop in class to make sure I understood the professor. If I didn't keep up or understand, she would come to my desk and work the problem out many times until she felt like I comprehended the material. She would go to the math lab with me to make sure I was able to complete the homework.

In addition, she would give me sample problems to work on, which I would complete for her by the next day. This process continued through Math 98. I didn't make straight A's, but I passed both of the classes with C's. I was just relieved to pass with a C, which meant I could progress to the next Math class. Unfortunately, the classes didn't count toward my degree, just toward my GPA.

Since I had used the buddy system successfully with her, I decided I was going to introduce myself to the smartest girls in every class I attended from now on. So I went to every class, sat in the front, and took notes on who made the highest grades on tests and assignments. I thought I was content with being a C student, until I saw the white girls quarrelling with the professor because they received a 95 on a test instead of 100. I thought to myself, *What the hell is wrong with them? I would be glad to take the 95. They would probably die if they had my score of 73.* At that very moment, I realized, like them, I too could be an "A" student. So, I walked up to the smart girls, introduced myself, and told them how impressed I was with their intelligence. I asked, *"Can I study with y'all? Is there any way I can learn how to study like y'all do?"* I never got no for an answer. I studied with the smart girls and worked extra hard to keep up with them. I would study for hours by myself before meeting to study with them. I wanted them to think I was as smart as they were.

They never knew I wasn't as smart as them and I always did whatever they asked. They opened my eyes to a whole new world. I had never even heard of Starbucks until I met them. They would bake muffins, cookies, and brownies for the study groups. I was in heaven. I worked really hard and went from making C's to A's. This was the best thing that had ever happened to me. Other students now considered me smart. The problem was that I wasn't naturally smart; I was smart enough to study hard enough to keep up. I had determined that failure was just not an option.

I realized I didn't have to be smart; I just had to be determined, motivated, and focused. This came with a high price tag for me. I had to change my thinking. I had to think like a smart person. I had to read, read, read, and then read some more. I had to give up clubbing, hanging out, staying up late, and going to movies—basically all my extra-curricular activities. In order for me to receive all As, I had to think like an A student, I had to surround myself with A students, and I did that consistently throughout my three years at Kennesaw State University.

Math wasn't my only weakness; writing was another. I could read well, but I couldn't write worth a dime. I took a Communication class where we had to write many papers. These were simple papers about whatever we chose to write about, but we had to read them in front of the class. Well, I would write about me, my life, my friends, etc. I loved to share my stories with the class.

One of the most painful moments for me was at the beginning of class. The professor would talk about how much she enjoyed reading the papers and how she graded them. Every time she got to my name, I would cringe in my chair, my knees would shake, and my eyes would burn with tears of disappointment. She would carefully hand me my papers folded so none of the students could see all the corrections she had made with her red marker. One day, my professor wrote a note that I should see her after class.

I waited until all the other students left. The professor said, *"Johnnetta, I am concerned about your writing. You cannot be successful in any career field you choose if you can't write."* She sat down beside me and went over some simple parts of speech that most students learn in the second and third grade. She gave me advice on how to shorten my long run-on sentences by simply adding a semi-colon to separate a thought. She taught me about subject and verb agreement and other rules of grammar. She said, *"You have an A paper, but because of all the grammatical errors I have to give you a C."* I left with tears in my eyes.

That evening, I purchased a dictionary, thesaurus, and MLA and APA style books to learn how to write. I went to the writing lab at least three times each week to get help with my writing. I was dedicated to becoming a better writer. I wasn't going to fail. I had mastered the streets, so I could surely master writing. After all, I needed to be able to write well in order to be taken seriously.

I made it through math and writing, but didn't do well in Biology, Pre-Calculus and Chemistry. I made a "D" and two "F's" in those classes. I didn't realize I was taking such difficult classes in one semester. It was not a wise decision.

My GPA hit rock bottom at a 1.50. I was devastated. I was doing great in my major classes, but not in my pre-requisite classes. This wasn't good enough. I had to pull up my grades. My dream of becoming a physical therapist was gradually fading. Another friend was studying to be a physical therapist at KSU as well. We met in Birmingham and she moved to the same apartment complex. She made an appointment for both of us to visit Emory's Physical Therapy Department, one of the best in the nation. We were so excited to be visiting the department. We would at least know our chances for acceptance into the program. After spending an evening at Emory touring the department, meeting other students, and listening to professors give mini-lectures on the GPA, GRE, and admission requirements, we knew if we were going to get accepted we had to work our asses off.

The next semester, I went to the Communication Department and changed my major from Health, Physical Education, and Science to Communication with a media concentration. I was happy. I loved to talk, so I thought this would be a piece a cake. Well, it wasn't easy, but the classes were fun and entertaining and I fit right in. I continued to study with all the smart white girls in my classes and pulled my grades back up. I began to write better. I took a senior advanced writing class, which I was nervous about. I turned in my assignments, and my professor would grade them and make notes for changes. Then he would give the papers back to me to make the corrections and return them to him for a final grade. One day I wrote a paper, turned it in, and got an "A." He made no corrections on my paper, no red ink, no suggestions, and no grammatical errors. The only comment on my paper was: "Excellent! Did you get any help?" I was so proud of myself. I wrote that paper alone without any help. At last, I could write a paper.

My final year was approaching and I had already applied for my graduation approval two semesters earlier. I had to find an internship before I could graduate. This was tough but exciting. I would picture myself picking up doughnuts and coffee for my intern staff. I wanted to be like Puff Daddy and his intern. I wanted to intern at MTV, the David Letterman Show, Oprah Winfrey, and on and on... but those internships required a GPA of at least 3.0 and I only had a 2.6. My grades killed that dream. I applied for an internship at a local radio station, the same station where Ludacris interned before he became a famous rapper. After weeks of not hearing anything back from the station, out of the blue one evening I received a phone call to come in for an interview. I was so thrilled. I didn't realize that a few hundred students were interviewed. The line was wrapped around two city blocks in front of the station. I was probably the only one there that was 35 years old. The interviews started at about 6 p.m. Someone would come down the elevator and ask for 10 to 15 people to come up in a group. I was in the last group to go up, at about 10 p.m. By the time they got to my group, they were only giving us about five minutes to introduce ourselves, without telling us this was going to be our only shot at getting a position. When they got to me, I boldly said, "My name is Johnnetta McSwain-Clay. I'm 35 and have recently moved from Birmingham, Alabama." I basically gave them a brief description of my life story. I could tell they were impressed. They listened to everyone and told us we would be hearing from them soon.

I didn't hear anything for a while. The semester ended and summer began. I was preparing for the Fourth of July, expecting about 10 guests, some driving from Birmingham. I got a phone call from someone asking if I could help out with a live remote for a well-known gospel radio personality at a major grocery store on the other side of town. I didn't want to leave my friends, nor did I want to go out in the heat. But I agreed to be there. I met up with the remote team at the station and we went to the grocery store. The producer showed me how to set up the remote station and told me to stand at the front of the store and hand out barbecued hot wings to the customers. A well-known maker of barbecue sauce was paying the radio station big bucks to promote their new barbecue flavor. I did exactly as I was told; however, it was hard telling black people they could only have one wing.

As I was standing there, I saw some of the familiar faces I had seen during the interview process staring at me the entire time. At last, the morning show host of the number one Gospel station in Atlanta approached me. She told me how impressed she was with my personality; how I took control of passing out those wings, and that she would like to see me Monday morning at 6 a.m. to be her morning show producer. I had landed my internship.

I had to buy both boys alarm clocks for school. They had to be outside to catch their buses at different times in the mornings and I wasn't going to be home to wake them and make sure they were up. I had to get up at 4:30 a.m. in order to be dressed and ready to leave the house at 5:20 to be at the station by 6:30 a.m. I really felt sorry for Jahleel; his bus came at 7:10 a.m., so he had to be up by 6:30 to be ready to catch his bus. He mastered setting his alarm clock and never missed his bus. On the other hand, RaShod's bus came at 7:50 a.m. and he barely made his bus. This went on for a year. I worked at my internship, and from there went straight to class, never missing a beat. The boys understood. They enjoyed the benefits of me working at the radio station. We had tickets to everything going on in Georgia. We went to plays, the Soul Circus, NBA games, parties, concerts, etc. I brought them all kinds of T-shirts, give-a-ways, food, and much more. Even though I had to work at many of the events, they were glad to go with me. They would help me and even bring some of their friends along. This was one of the greatest times of my life. I met celebrities such as Lisa Ray, Bruce Bruce, Paula White, Tichina Arnold, and many more. I had the opportunity to work an exclusive live red carpet remote and attend the Triumph Awards. The night was simply "bling-bling."

GRADUATION:
I DID IT!

After I finished my internship and completed all the requirements, I was ready to graduate from KSU in May of 2006. I was thrilled; I couldn't believe three years had gone by that fast. The time had come. Finally, I was going to be wearing the black cap and gown that I had been trying on in the bookstore at the beginning of every semester. This is what motivated me the most. I paid for my cap and gown, ordered invitations, and sent them out to family and friends. I had a house full of supporters. The day had arrived.

We were lined up by last name. I saw thousands of people looking for their loved ones that were graduating. I was looking around for my family and friends. I wondered where they were sitting.

Finally, after about a hundred names were called, I heard "Johnnetta McSwain, Bachelor of Science." I walked on to the stage as if I were receiving an Oscar Award. I couldn't believe all my long hours of studying, countless nights in the Writing Lab, endless hours in the Math Lab, traveling 45 miles one way to school four days per week, full-time classes each semester, working 35 hours each week at my internship, long lines in the bookstore, headaches from writing a thesis, struggling to make ends meet with no job, repossession of a car, marital problems, hundreds of cups of Starbucks coffee, daily energy drinks, and sacrificing everything and everyone had finally paid off.

I felt relieved, accomplished, proud, and happy; and at last, I felt valued. I had imagined when the day came, I would scream, kick, and cry profusely when my name was called. Instead, I walked across the stage in silence and disbelief. I could see flashes from my friends' cameras. I even saw smiles from my professors.

Finally, my mother was going to see one of her children make something of her life. She would no longer have to be ashamed of both of her children. She could now brag about what her child was doing. What made me most proud of was crossing that stage with my sons looking on. I had become a living example of the importance of going to college and the value of education. They would be able to look back and understand all the sacrifices I made and the reasons I made them. They would view me as a role model. They would tell their friends they had a role model and that getting an education was a requirement in their home.

PART 7

THE MASTER'S

CAN'T STOP HERE:
APPLYING FOR GRADUATE SCHOOL

During my preparation for graduation, I started praying and asking God to lead and guide me toward the direction I needed to be heading. I had begun the long, tedious process of preparing for graduate school. I was trying to find out what was I going to study for my master's degree. By this time, I knew I wanted to be a role model for other women like myself. I wanted women to know they can change their circumstances. Janice had already started her application process for the Clark Atlanta University, Whitney M. Young, Jr., School of Social Work program. I was helping her by reading over her admissions statement. As I did this, I thought more and more about my passion—what did I really want to do?

I knew I wanted to help women, so I started Googling occupations that support other women. To my surprise, I found social work jobs and social work graduate programs. That's when I began researching the Master's of Social Work (MSW). I had a little information from Janice, so I learned more about the program, the careers, and the money. I couldn't imagine being a social worker. I was not going to be wearing brown stockings, blue and black shoes, and blue and brown suits. I was a diva. I was not going to be working for the Department of Family and Children (DFACS), knocking on doors and taking people's children. No, not me. No matter what I Googled, I was led right back to all the occupations I could do with an MSW. I told Janice about what I had found and she encouraged me to apply to the same program as her at Clark Atlanta. She told me how easy it would be to attend a historically black college or university (HBCU). Since I had gotten a good education from KSU, I would be more than prepared to excel in the master's program.

In order to get accepted for the fall semester, the application for the program was due by March of 2006. I started the long process of writing the eight-page autobiography that was part of the admission process. I still had a fear of writing. I needed help, so I went back to the writing lab for assistance with my sentence structure, punctuation, and grammar. I spent long hours at the writing lab revising what I had previously written weeks before. After several weeks, I finally got the approval to submit my statement to the admissions team at CAU. I completed the entire package and dropped it off in person. I wanted them to remember me by my face, not by a number.

The hard part wasn't over; I still had to take my General Requirement Exam. This exam is a standardized test that enables schools to rate academic ability. It helps universities pick the best applicants for their programs. I didn't do well on my test despite having studied for a long time. This was the hardest test I had ever taken in my life and the most important one. I thought the General Education Degree (GED) was hard, but it had nothing on the GRE. I submitted my low score anyway, hoping my admissions statement would make up for what I was lacking.

CAU ACCEPTANCE

Three months had come and gone, and by June, I still had not received a letter informing me of my fate. The program was scheduled in August, so I was frustrated, worried, anxious, and impatient. I had not applied to another school and everything I had was riding on me getting into the MSW program at CAU. I knew I needed a master's degree to make any kind of real money and to be taken seriously at my age. My 10-year plan was to receive my bachelor's, master's, and doctorate degrees, and nothing was going to stop me. Failure was not an option.

One sunny, hot day in June, I opened the door and saw my son take a white envelope out of the mailbox. I could see the CAU logo on the envelope from where I was standing on the porch, about 20 feet away. At that moment, I knew whatever was in that envelope was going to change the rest of my life—whether I was accepted or not. If I was accepted my life would change dramatically. I would then be the first in my family to have a master's degree, I would have credentials behind my name, and I would be a licensed professional. Finally,

I would get some respect and feel more valued. I started to panic. RaShod immediately opened the letter. By the time he re-entered the house, he had read the letter.

"On behalf of the faculty of the Whitney M. Young, Jr. School of Social Work (WMYJSSW) at Clark Atlanta University (CAU), I am pleased to accept your application for full-time enrollment in the 2006-2007 entering class of the Masters of Social Work Program. Your acceptance into the program is based upon your academic record, personal statement, and letters of reference that speak to your character, commitment to serve others, and your potential ability to do graduate work."

I couldn't believe what I was reading. I was accepted. I fell down to the floor and started to cry. I started thanking God and everybody who had helped me prepare for this moment. I e-mailed all my friends who came by to celebrate with wine and food.

MENTOR:
SUSAN KOSSAK

The remainder of June and all of July went by in a blur. Suddenly, it was August. I had been running around on campus trying to make sure all my financial aid was approved. Clark is a private school and the tuition is very costly. Without financial aid, I could not afford to attend. I have to admit Clark campus was a hot-ass, ghetto fabulous mess! When I first walked on campus, it was a cultural shock. After three years at KSU, I had become accustomed to a lush green campus with stately buildings and a surplus of amenities. Most of the students at KSU were white and laid back. In contrast, many of the younger students at CAU were loud and alley. Some women wore mini-skirts, Daisy Dukes, low-cut tops, four-inch stilettos, long multi-color weaves and braids. They also carried "What the hell you looking at?" attitudes. Some brothers had on baggy jeans hanging off their asses, white T's and hats, chains and gold teeth. I smelled the smoke from the ribs, polish sausage, and hamburgers cooking on the large barbecue grills on the corner. Vendors sold fake *Gucci*, *Louis Vuitton*, and *Chanel* bags, glasses, hats, and scarves.

Greek colors and step shows lined the streets surrounding the three colleges: Clark, Spellman, and Morehouse. I have to be honest, I felt right at home. I was truly honored to have a chance to experience a HBCU. I could fully appreciate the opportunity to experience both a predominately white school and a historically black school. I felt like I had the best of both worlds.

My four classes were all in one building on Monday and Tuesdays, from 9 a.m. to 4 p.m. I had to do my internship on Wednesdays and Thursdays. During orientation, the staff introduced themselves and explained the criteria of the program to us.

One professor, in particular, stood out to me, Dr. Susan Kossak. Dr. Kossak is a slender, white, Jewish, middle-aged, jazzy, beautiful woman. I thought to myself—*What the hell can a white woman teach all these black students in this program? What can she possibly teach me? I'm sure she's never been to the hood.* Every time I saw her, she was in a hurry.

One day, I was sitting in the cafeteria and she walked up to me and started talking about the story I had written for admission. She told me I had an amazing background and needed to be helping other women by sharing my story. I couldn't believe she cared enough to stop and tell me that. That was the day my life changed forever. She was that angel I had prayed for. I had asked God to send me someone who would accept me and help me get my story out to other women. I asked God for someone who wasn't going to be intimidated by me, would love me unconditionally, and would help me unselfishly.

I took three of Dr. Kossak's classes, so we got to know each other pretty well. I would visit her office and sit with her and we would talk socially as well as professionally about everything. She would ask questions about my life. One particular question she asked me quite often was, "What's your bottom line? Why did you really change your life?"

We met almost weekly in her office and discussed my story. We became really close. I had started thinking about applying to some schools for my doctorate degree. I was thinking about studying Public Health, since it went so well with my social work degree. I spoke with some of my classmates who were graduating before me. They were talking about which schools they were applying to after graduation. One student mentioned Harvard School of Public Health. She went on to talk about how she was thinking about applying to Harvard, but she didn't want to move. So, I thought, *I can go to Harvard.* I saw Dr. Kossak and told her, "I am applying to Harvard and I need your help." She accepted my offer and hugged my neck.

It was around March of 2007 that I started the long, painstaking process of applying to Harvard. I started researching the program and the school. I called the school to build a rapport with the professors in the program. The application didn't have to be in until October of 2007 in order to be accepted for fall classes in August of 2008. I started working day and night on my admissions statement. Dr. Kossak would read over my statement and give it back to me with every other word circled in red. Oh, my God, I felt like I was back at Kennesaw State. But failure had stopped being an option long ago. It didn't matter whether I got accepted; what mattered was that I wanted to do something no one in my family or circle had done. I was living for other women. I wanted to reach for things people said I couldn't reach for because I wasn't smart enough, couldn't write well enough, or just wasn't good enough.

Dr. Kossak did not teach that summer and underwent foot surgery, but she never missed meeting me at her office every week to help with my admissions statement. I would see her limping on crutches, trying to make it across the street to the building with her foot wrapped up. She always smiled when she saw me. She never complained. She made me feel like I could do anything. She never looked down on me. She allowed me to be myself. If I spoke incorrect English she would correct me graciously but most of the time she would just let me talk. She understood where I was coming from. She even allowed me to teach her some Ebonics.

We worked for six months on my admission statement and wrote a 30-page article for publication at the same time. Finally, she put her approval on the admission statement, saying it was good enough to submit to Harvard. I was studying for the GRE to get a higher score; my previous score was too low for Harvard. I called the contact person for the program I was applying for and reserved my spot for the open house. I didn't know how I was going to come up with the money to fly to Boston, but I was going to get there one way or another. I made appointments to meet with the admissions panel, the housing director and students, and planned to sit in on some lectures. I called everyone I knew and asked them to help me get to Harvard. A few friends gave me enough money to pay for a round-trip ticket and hotel.

I was nervous in the airport. I started to think, *Who am I fooling? I'm not Harvard material. What would I really do if they accept me? A poor black girl from the hood?* I went through the metal detector and was asked to step out of the line to be searched. I forgot I couldn't go through airport security with over three ounces of toiletries; I had eight ounces of everything. I had to throw it all away and get back in line. By the time I got to my terminal, my plane was getting ready to take off and they wouldn't let me board it. I was so upset. If I didn't make it on that plane, I would get to Boston too late to make all my appointments. I went to the desk and asked the customer service rep about the next plane to Boston. I told her I was going to Harvard and I couldn't miss my flight. She was so impressed she said, *"Stand by, let me see what I can do for you."* She called me back over to the desk and said, "We have an extra seat in the business class, but you have to pay an extra $50 for the seat."

I replied, "I don't have any extra money. I only have enough to eat at a McDonald's."

She smiled and offered.

"Get on the plane, and go get them for me."

I thanked her and ran onto the plane.

Sitting in business class was just like first class—big leather seats, alcoholic beverages, and food. I made it to Boston and was greeted by a team of Harvard professionals. I visited lectures, chatted with students, and met with the director of the program. It was one of the greatest experiences of my life. I had gone to Harvard. I didn't get accepted, but I did gain something bigger than myself. I had an experience I could share with women to let them know nothing is impossible if you believe. I was so relieved and glad the entire experience was over. I had accomplished a lot.

Spring of 2008 finally arrived and it was time to get approval for graduation. It was hectic trying to make sure I had completed all my graduation requirements. Things were much more disorganized at CAU than KSU. I finally paid all my graduation fees and picked up my cap and gown from the bookstore. I had been so busy finishing up my conceptual paper in order to graduate and applying for graduate schools, I didn't have time to be excited about graduating.

I invited my momma, sister, and close friends to the ceremonies—the Hooding ceremony and the Graduation ceremony. Both were beautiful. Momma and Sonya came to see me walk across the stage. It was indeed a wonderful feeling to have them both there. For some reason, I wasn't as excited this go-around as I had been two years before. I guess I was tired and burned out. I just wanted to get it over with. I had been in school for five years straight with no breaks.

PART 8

THE "12 STEPS"

FACING MY FEARS:
WRITING AGAIN

While still attending Clark Atlanta, one day I visited Dr. Kossak at her office. She took a piece of paper off her desk and gently placed it in my hand. "Look this over," she said. It was a workshop proposal for the National Association of Social Workers (NASW), Georgia Chapter. The NASW is the largest organization for Social Workers. Dr. Kossak encouraged me to join the organization at the student rate and write my life story in a workshop format. I took the paper home and read it carefully. I didn't want to tell her that I was afraid to write. I knew I wasn't a good writer. She didn't know how much she intimidated me when I was around her. She is the smartest person I have ever met in my life. She knows everything. She is so smart and articulate. She is funny and as real as real can be. She has allowed me to be me and never asks me to change the way I dress, act, or speak. When I was a student, she always sat quietly and attentively listened to my every word. She comforted me and cried with me when I needed to cry.

A fellow classmate was a recovering crack addict. We shared the same internship, so she had heard me talk about my life and where I came from. One day she asked me the strangest question, "How long have you been in recovery?" I was shocked, wondering why she would ask me a question like that. Did I look like an addict? I surely knew all about addiction. I asked why she asked me such an odd question, and she said, "Hearing your story, it seems like you have been working through the *12 Steps*."

That night, I began researching the *12 Steps*. I printed them out and started reading them and comparing them to my life. It suddenly dawned on me, *I will write my life story in the format of a 12-Step module*. I realized there was no 12-Step program out there for women like me. I was not a substance-abuse addict. I was not addicted to alcohol, sex, and gambling—but I was an addict. I was an addict of the streets. So I turned on my computer and typed up the 12-Step Self-Awareness Model (SAM). I called Dr. Kossak at home and told her about the *12 Steps* and she said, "That's it! Let's do it."

I took it to her the next day; she critiqued the steps and perfected the module. She, another professor, and I worked on the proposal and abstract for the NASW workshop. We sent in the proposal with Dr. Kossak being the lead presenter and contact person so we would have a greater chance of acceptance. Before the end of the spring semester, we received approval for the workshop. I was ecstatic. We had until October to prepare for the presentation and worked hard to get it together.

We had about 60 attendees register for "Breaking Negative Cycles: Beating the Odds." Dr. Kossak opened the workshop, briefly introducing me. I presented my life story through the *12 Steps* and the third presenter discussed the theory behind the story. At the end of the workshop, everyone rose to their feet and gave a standing ovation. I was amazed by the reaction to our presentation; some people cried, some had loss of words, others asked personal and professional questions, and still others came up just to hug and congratulate me.

At that very moment, I knew my calling: I had to spread my story in order to help save other women like me. We were so thrilled with the success of the workshop that we decided to do something more with these *12 Steps*.

A few days passed when Dr. Kossak and I received numerous e-mails from some of the workshop attendees asking for our help. Some wanted Dr. Kossak to be their mentor. Some wanted to know if I could come speak at their company, church, or organization. Dr. Kossak stated she had done many workshops in her career, but had never experienced a reaction that was received from ours. So I suggested, *"We have to do something. Let's redo the workshop, but this time, we'll video tape it and put it on a DVD."*

Dr. Kossak called CAU-TV and made an appointment to meet with the professor who handles video recording. We met and set up a time and date to do the taping in the CAU-TV studio. I was really excited. I knew this would be something I could give to people and sell for profit.

In January of 2008, we taped the entire workshop the way we did it at the conference. I invited my best friends, along with a few students to sit in the audience, and it went great. We now discovered a way to get our message out to women everywhere.

Self-Awareness Model (SAM): 12 Steps

The Self-Awareness Model (SAM) is an intervention tool used with women that teaches them to overcome and triumph over unforeseeable and extraordinary circumstances in life by breaking those negative cycles that cripple and impede one's ability to beat the odds. Those introduced to this SAM will be empowered to release unconscious, hurtful scripts and connect to inner/personal energies that lead to recovery and truth in our conscious lives. Individuals will learn self-discovery, acceptance, and release of past traumatic histories, and self-sustaining skills to grow and succeed. In turn this SAM and the subsequent skills gained can be taught to individuals, empowering them to break the vicious cycles that hold them hostage.

THE 12 STEPS

1. **Becoming self aware and admitting there are cycles in our life**

   - **Family Generational Cycle**
        Intimate Relationship Cycle
        Friendship Cycle
        Environmental Cycle
        Victim Blaming Cycle
        Mental Cycle
     Abuse (sexual, mental, physical and self)
     Education
     Drugs

   - **Intimate Relationship Cycle**
     - Attracting the wrong/same kind of men
     - Being needy/unable to say NO
     - Claiming, "He will change"
     - Staying in a bad relationship
     - Justifying, "But, this is my baby's daddy"
     - Saying, "It's too hard to find a man"
     - Rationalizing, "But we have been together so long"

   - **Friendship Cycle**
     - Having the same old kind of friends
     - Keeping jealous friends
     - Retaining good friends/bad friends/childhood friends
     - Determining how to be a friend
     - Choosing friends
     - Picking new friends

   - **Environmental Cycle**
     - Being a product of your environment
     - Justifying, "Because this is the way I was raised/taught; it's my family's tradition"
     - Relocating from your environment (drugs & violence)
     - Choosing better neighborhood/community (housing)

- Finding better opportunities (school, career, positive experiences, and quality of life)

- **Victim Blaming Cycle**
  - Claiming, "Because this happened to me, I can't..."
  - Justifying, "It's your fault/if it wasn't for you..."
  - Feeling, "Nobody loves me anyway"
  - Thinking—"The world owes me"
  - Saying, "The MAN got me down"
  - Rationalizing, "I can't do it; why should I do it?"

- **Mental Cycle**
  - Discover the traumas buried deep down inside us
  - Be able to forgive unconditionally in order to gain closure and move on
  - Let go of the past and everybody that is involved in it
  - Think positively; surround yourself with positiveness
  - Know failure should not be an option
  - Stop holding on to hate and revenge; it will keep you down
  - Stop being the victim; you are your biggest enemy
  - Stop blaming yourself for things out of your control
  - Stop re-living your childhood
  - Embrace the saying, "You cannot do anything about your childhood but you can do something about your adulthood"
  - Change your way of thinking; if you do not change your mental environment you cannot change your physical environment.
  - Stop running from reality—it will catch up with you when you least expect it

2. **Becoming aware of your environment**
   - If you never leave your environment, you stay the same and do the same
   - If you cannot see outside your environment, you will remain stuck

3. **Becoming aware that you do not have to be the victim**
   - You were beaten, sexually assaulted, mistreated, or not loved
   - You didn't finish school; you are not smart; you can't keep up
   - You believe it's just too hard
   - You are not as strong as someone else
   - You have children
   - You are too old; it's no use
   - You have no support

4. **Becoming aware that you do not have to be POOR**
   - Your entire family is poor
   - You make minimum wages; you are struggling to make ends meet
   - You think, "Going to school is a waste of time. What good is a degree?"
   - You believe, "Somebody has to be poor"
   - You say, "I don't need to be rich"

5. **Becoming aware that you don't have to be what people say you are going to be**
   - "You will never be anything"
   - "Nobody wants you but me"
   - "You will never change"
   - "You will be back, you won't make it"
   - "I failed, so will you"
   - "You are not good enough/smart enough"
   - "You're just dreaming, it's not possible"
   - "Nobody I know has accomplished anything"

6. **Becoming aware there are injustices in the world but that we can still rise above these obstacles and become successful**
   - You are a woman
   - You are a woman of color

- You didn't finish school
- You do not fit in
- You are poor
- You cannot attend the best schools/universities/colleges
- Society says you can't

7. **Becoming aware that we are women of strength, who stand for survival, empowerment, motherhood, leadership, love, nurturing, beauty, respect, and courage to overcome anything**
   - You had children out of wedlock
   - You have more than one baby daddy
   - You're living off the system (welfare, food stamps/Section 8/housing projects/Medicaid etc.)
   - You have been in bad/violent relationships
   - You have been incarcerated
   - You do not fit the description of a model
   - You are too fat, dark, tall, short, ugly or slow
   - You have been evicted/jobless/careless
   - You have lost all hope
   - You didn't grow up with two parents, good parents, or any parents
   - You didn't grow up with a silver spoon in your mouth

8. **Becoming aware of your worth**
   - You are beautiful
   - You deserve to be loved
   - You are raising your children the best you can/the best you know how
   - You don't need a man to complete you, lay down next to you, or provide for you financially
   - You don't need a man to define you
   - You are a survivor
   - You don't have to accept anything less than the best
   - You deserve R-E-S-P-E-C-T
   - You should be treated like the queen you are

9. **Becoming aware of your fear of failure or success**
   - "Because I might just be successful, then what?"
   - "What good is it going to do me anyway?"
   - "I am afraid of what people will think or say about me"
   - "I am too old, there's no hope for me"
   - "I am not smart enough"
   - "I have been at my job so long I can't do anything else"
   - "I have too many bills"
   - "I don't have the time"
   - "I don't need an education"
   - "I already have enough, I'm fine"

10. **Becoming aware of negative influences in your life**
    - Yourself
    - Bad thinking
    - Bad environment
    - Bad family members
    - Bad friends
    - Bad relationships
    - Bad jobs

11. **Becoming aware of change**
    - Thinking, "I don't want to or need to change"
    - Claiming, "I like it just the way it is"
    - Rationalizing, "It's too hard to find a good man/job"
    - Feeling, "It is easier to live off the SYSTEM"
    - Saying, "I have been like this all my life"
    - Changing your attitude, your way of thinking
    - Knowing that change is good
    - Understanding that life brings on changes
    - Realizing that you don't have to face reality, it will face you
    - Embracing that it's never too late to change; you are never too old to change

12. **Becoming aware of your inner strength to change your past, to overcome traumatic obstacles, and to break barriers of self-destruction**
    - You don't have to continue your path of self- destruction
    - You don't have to repeat your past cycles
    - You don't have to breed hate and anger
    - You don't need to be an abuser because you were abused
    - You don't have to give up and die
    - Life goes on
    - Happiness is obtainable
    - **Love is real**
        - Forgiveness is divine
    - **Hope is alive**
        - Success and prosperity are reachable
    - **Dreams are achievable**
        - Believing is receiving
    - **Attitude is King in the battle to success**
        - Life is worth living and you can live well!

FINALLY FORGIVING
MOMMA

A lexander Pope wrote: "To err is human, to forgive is divine." I learned this as a child. But how could I forgive my mother when she did nothing to protect my sister and me? I began to pray to God and ask for his forgiveness for my own sins first, and then I began to ask God to give me understanding, compassion, and sympathy for my mother, so I could start the forgiving process.

First, I had to accept that what happened to me was out of my control. I had absolutely no control over my childhood, but I have 100% control over my adulthood. Next, I had to understand that my mother could not love and protect Sonya and me, because she simply didn't know how. No one had shown her. She could not give us what she didn't have. Growing up in the house with her daddy, whom she called "The Awful Old Man," her mother had stood by and allowed him to sexually abuse her and her sisters as little girls. In confidence, she would describe the evil acts of her daddy to her mother, but then he would whoop them both for discussing it. She recalls her daddy beating her mother to a bloody pulp in front of their children. She vowed she would never let any man put his hands on her. "I swore to God I would kill a man that put his hands on me, I would never let a man hit me. This is why I was so mean and tough toward men." Her mother had instilled this horrible family generational tradition: Don't talk about it to anyone.

Momma dropped out of high school and left home at 16 to stay in a motel with a man much older than she was. That man turned out to be my daddy. She, too, looked for love and protection in the streets. She didn't plan on getting pregnant. Her momma had never told her about her body or the dangers of sex. Maybe this is why she told Sonya and me that the stork brings babies. She would always tell us she didn't want babies. All she wanted to do was have fun. Nevertheless, she gave birth to Sonya at age 19, and then gave birth to me 11 months later. When she was six months pregnant with me, Aretha Franklin's *Ain't No Way* was popular. She would listen to that song and cry.

As I got older, I started understanding why my momma was so bitter, angry, and mean. Why couldn't she just love me, and hug me, and tell me how I was her little queen? Why didn't she protect me from my uncles and the other men? Why did she tell me she wished I had died? Why didn't she just listen to us when we were trying to tell her about the sexual abuse? Why didn't she stand up for us, when people in the church put us down? Why couldn't she show up to my school plays, graduations, the birth of my two sons, and the custody battle of my youngest son in court? Why didn't she tell me to stay in high school and go to college? It took me a long time to find the answers. The reason is because she did not love herself. Momma was never taught how to love herself or anyone else. She had no one positive in her life to emulate. She was never protected from the men in her family. When I asked her why she didn't want me or love me, she said, *"There was a time I didn't love myself. I wanted to die. I felt like I wasn't any good or of any use to anyone."*

After I had gotten my first one-bedroom apartment at the age of 23, I invited my mother over on Mother's Day to eat dinner with me and the boys. I wanted to confront Momma to let her know what had really happened to Sonya and me, and how it had destroyed us. As we sat down to eat, I brought up the abuse. She got very angry and started shouting, *"I don't want to hear it. Just shut up. I didn't come over here to be put down,"* and so on. She went on to say how she did her best to take care of us, and what happened to us was no fault of hers. She got up and left. I never even got to tell her everything that happened.

That is when I decided that if she would never hear me out, my children had a slim chance of having a relationship with my mother, and I would never get to have a mother-daughter relationship with her. I had gotten so anesthetized to the pain, I didn't care anymore if she ever called or came around again. I was done trying to love her. I had never gotten a birthday, Christmas, or any kind of card or present. In return, I never bought her anything. This was normal in our family. She hardly came over to see the boys, though she would buy gifts for them. She did love them the best way she could. There were several other times my sister and I tried to have a sit-down talk with my momma, but she would always walk out on us without admitting anything or ever saying she was sorry.

When I relocated and started school, I began to learn how some of the things that happened to her and her momma could be learned behavior. I called her and set some boundaries in our relationship. I told her I would no longer accept it when she called me a *bitch* and a *ho*. I would no longer be verbally and emotionally abused, nor would my children. I told her this was the end of the road.

"If you want to be a grandmomma, here's your second chance to be a better momma to them than you were to me."

I started saying, "I love you" at the end of every phone call, until she began saying it back to me. I started hugging her every time

I saw her, and she started hugging me back.

When I was getting married, Momma and Sonya came to the bridal shower. We made a pallet on the floor, lied down together, and watched movies. Then it happened. Sonya and I begged Momma to hear us out. We told her everything that happened to us in raw detail—all the abuse, everything that hurt us from childhood to adulthood. Momma started crying. For the first time, she listened to everything. We all cried uncontrollably. But, we still didn't get an apology or an admittance of any wrongdoing on her part. My sister would get so angry, because Momma wouldn't admit to her mistakes. Sonya would sometimes cuss Momma out and then go back to drugs. There were times she would get so depressed—she would attempt suicide and would have to go to the mental ward.

God willing, I had to forgive Momma. In order for me to live and be a good momma to my boys, I had to finally forgive her; for myself; for my own peace of mind; for my own sanity.

At this point, I had learned how to love myself, my boys, and everything about my life. There was no need to hate Momma any longer. What good was that going to do? I never told my boys anything bad about Momma—they loved her. I knew she loved me in her own strange way.

Growing up, I am sure Momma expressed that she loved me somehow; however, the first time I remember her saying, "I love you," was when I was in my early 30's.

THE DOCUMENTARY:
THE ROAD BEYOND ABUSE

B ecause of the overwhelming response to the first *12-Step Self-Awareness Model* (SAM) workshop in October of 2007, Dr. Kossak and I knew we had something special and had to do more with the *12 Steps*. Dr. Kossak called the *Atlanta Journal Constitution*, radio stations, and Georgia Public Broadcasting (GPB). She spent hours calling and telling people about my story and how we needed to get it out in the media. She spoke to Pamela Roberts, an executive producer, who was working on a documentary with an emphasis on child abuse and neglect. Dr. Kossak invited her to meet me at school. We met and talked and Ms. Roberts decided to profile my life story in the documentary. I was flabbergasted. A few weeks later, we started taping the documentary, beginning with the January 2008 re-taping of the 12-Step SAM workshop for the DVD. I never thought it would be much work, but it was tedious. I now have a newfound respect for actors.

We went back to Birmingham to tape the neighborhoods I grew up in, the night clubs, my high school, the infamous house, and much more. We did interviews with some of my previous professors on campus at Kennesaw State and with Dr. Kossak at Clark Atlanta. I had called my sister and asked her if she wanted to be a part of the documentary. She didn't hesitate for the opportunity to tell her story; however, I didn't ask my momma. I knew it was going to be too hard for her to talk about and relive what happened. Instead, Pam called her and asked if she wanted to participate. She agreed and they made a second trip to Birmingham to interview her alone, which surprised me.

We worked on the documentary throughout the year. It was hard for me to juggle working on the film, attending graduate school full-time, going to my internship three days each week, and being a full-time "Momma." It was very difficult at times to re-enact what my sister and I had lived through, especially revisiting the house where the abuse took place after all these years. Sitting on the same front porch, where I was made to sit naked in the cold was exceed-ingly distressing to experience again. When Sonya walked into the house, she was so overwhelmed that she started crying liberally. My momma said, "I am not going in that house. Things happened in that house." She walked in the front yard and on the side of the house, before she sat back in the vehicle and waited for us to wrap up taping. She never went inside.

After long hours of filming, crying, laughing, and bonding, on April 15, 2009, the documentary, *The Road Beyond Abuse*, debuted on Georgia Public Broadcasting. The documentary consisted of about an hour-long segment of my story, and that of a young white man. Then, it featured an hour-long panel discussion covering the issues of child abuse and neglect from various professionals. I invited my friends over to my house and we all gathered around the television to watch. There wasn't a dry eye in the room. Friends and viewers started to ring my phone incessantly.

A couple of days later, Kennesaw State University held a

special debut and invited all my professors, friends, family, and community to celebrate. They were so proud of me. My mother and sister came to see the documentary, because it was not released in Alabama. They looked beautiful. Both of them wore new dresses, and someone had given Sonya shoes and fixed her hair. At the KSU debut, they both sat down in the very front of the auditorium where everyone could see them, and not one time did they lower their heads in shame. They were empowered. It took a lot of guts to come and face their shame in front of the whole audience. They got a standing ovation.

RaShod had arrived from the Air Force and Jahleel was close by. It was one of the best times of my life, seeing my entire family in one room for a cause.

This documentary has opened up a lot of wounds, but it has also started a journey of forgiveness and healing for my family. I just hope it does the same for other families.

I was both proud and honored to be a major part of *The Road Beyond Abuse*. In June of 2010, it was nominated and won the Southeast Regional Emmy® Award for Best Topical Documentary.

To watch *The Road Beyond Abuse* visit:
www.GPB.com/road-beyond-abuse

Visit YouTube.com to see my story in three parts.

EPILOGUE
TODAY

Since graduating from Clark Atlanta University with a Master's of Social Work in May of 2008, Johnnetta has been presenting her copyrighted 12-Step Self-Awareness Model (SAM) in local and national conferences and professional workshops.

In July of 2008, she launched *Breaking the Cycle: Beating the Odds* (BCBO); an organization that empowers women to become self-aware of their negative, addictive behavioral cycles, which cripple their ability to reach for their fullest potential in life.

Johnnetta has been busy managing a team of volunteers for BCBO. She is currently presenting her most requested workshop, *12-Step Self-Awareness Model (SAM),* nationally. In addition, she is writing and creating new, dynamic workshops and trainings to present in conferences worldwide.

Johnnetta McSwain is sought for speaking engagements at churches, schools, colleges, and conferences. She is currently enrolled at Clark Atlanta University pursuing her Ph.D. in Social Work, becoming the first in her family with a doctorate. In addition, she is currently working on her second book, *Breaking My Silence and Finally Letting Go of the Shame.* This book will be a compilation of triumphant stories of women who have beaten the odds in their lives.

For more information on upcoming workshops, conferences, trainings, books, and book signings, please visit Johnnetta's websites at:

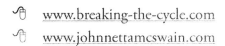

    www.breaking-the-cycle.com

    www.johnnettamcswain.com

Contact Johnnetta McSwain at:
Johnnetta McSwain
c/o Breaking the Cycle: Beating the Odds
P.O. Box 1914; Powder Springs, GA. 30127

Resources

There are an estimated 39 million survivors of child sexual abuse in America today (1)

Help Break the Silence of Abuse

1 in 4 girls and **1 in 6 boys** are **sexually abused** before their 18th birthdays (17, 20, 25, 28, 37, 74)

The **median age for reported sexual abuse is 9 years** old (64)

Approximately **20% of the victims of sexual abuse** are under age 8 (76)

Most **child victims never report the abuse** (33, 43, 44, 77)

Children's Advocacy Centers provide child-friendly, safe places for abused children and their families to seek help. To find a center near you:

Contact the **National Children's Alliance** - www.nca-online.org or call 1-800-239-9950

Some states require that anyone with suspicions of abuse report it. Information about each state's reporting requirements is available at **The National Clearinghouse on Child Abuse and Neglect** website: http://nccanch. acfhhs.gov/

Many states have too-free lines that accept reports of abuse from the entire state. To find out where to make a report in your state, identify the Child Abuse Reporting Numbers at **The National Clearinghouse on Child Abuse and Neglect** website: http://nccanch.acf.hhs.gov/ topics/reporting/guidelines.cfm

If the legal system does not provide adequate protection for a child, visit the **National Center for Victims of Crime** at: www.ncvc.org or call 1-800-FYI-CALL

Have staff specifically trained to deal with questions about suspected child sexual abuse. Call **Darkness to Light's** helpline, 1-866-FOR-LIGHT to be routed to resources in your community. www.darkness2light.org

Child help- USA National Child Abuse Hotline, 1-800-4-A-CHILD. http://www.childhelpusa.org
Stop It Now! - is a prevention organization with expertise in issues pertaining to perpetrators and older youth who are potential offenders. Go to www.stopitnow.com Or call 1-888-PREVENT

National Coalition Against Domestic Violence (NCADV) - helps survivors in all 50 states obtain comprehensive domestic violence program information quickly, provides domestic violence advocates with education and forums to build their programs' effectiveness, and serves as the forceful voice in Washington, DC, to lobby on behalf of shelters and domestic violence prevention programs. Go to www.ncadv.org

National Network to End Domestic Violence (NNEDV FUND)-The mission of the National Network to End Domestic Violence Fund is to create a social, political and economic environment in which violence against women no longer exists. Go to www.nnedv.org

Rape, Abuse, and Incest National Network (RAINN) - The Rape, Abuse & Incest National Network (RAINN) is the nation's largest anti-sexual assault organization, RAINN operates the National Sexual Assault hotline at 1-800-656-hope. And carries out programs to prevent sexual assault, help victims and ensure that rapist are brought to justice. Go to www.rainn.org

US Department of Justice Office on Violence Against Women- Site includes information about Sate-by-State OVW Grant Activities, information about Sexual Assault, Publications, Press Releases and Remarks, State Administering Agencies and more. Go to www.ojp.usdoj.gov/vawo

Women Against Domestic Violence (WADV) - WADV, Inc. is a group of women from across the world that has joined together in the struggle against domestic violence. WADV are here to help all of those affected by abuse. Go to www.wadv.org

Angels That Care- Domestic violence, missing/abused children/adults resource site. Covers all of USA and International. Go to www.angelsthatcare.org

Stop Abuse For Everyone (SAFE) - Stop Abuse For Everyone is a human rights organization that provides for battered men, same sex victims, teens, the elderly, and immigrants. Go to www.safe4all.org/info

Albel, G., Beker, J., Mittelman, M. Cunningham-Rathner, J., Rouleau, J., & Murphy, W. (1987). Self reported sex crimes on non-incarcerated paraphiliacs. *Journal of Interpersonal Violence*, 2(1), 3-25.

Doll, L.S., Koenig, L.J., & Purcell, D.W. (2004). Child sexual abuse and adult sexual risk: Where are we now? In L.S. Doll, S.O. O'Leary, L.J. Loening, & W. Pequegnat (Eds.) *From child sexual abuse to adult sexual risk* (pp. 3-10). Washington, DC: American Psychological Association.

Dube, S.R., Anda, R.F., Whitfield, C.L., Brown D. W. Felitti, V. J., Doug, M., & Giles, W.H. (2005). Long-term consequences of child hood sexual abuse by gender of victim. *American Journal of Preventive Medicine*, 28, 430-438.

(25) Fergusson. D., Horwood, L., & Lynskey, M. (1997). Childhood sexual abuse, adolescent sexual behavior, and sexual revictimization. *Child Abuse & Neglect*, 21, 789-80.

(28) Finkelhor, D., & Dziuba-Leatherman, J. (1994). Children as victims of violence: A national survey. *Pediatrics*, 94, 413-420.

(33) Goodman, G.S., Ghetti, S., Quas, J.A., Edelstein, R. S., Alexander, K. W., Redlich, A. D., Cordon, I. M., & Jones, D. P. H. (2003). A prospective study of memory for child sexual abuse: New findings relevant to the repressed-memory controversy.

(37) Hopper. J. (1998). *Child Abuse: Statistics, Research, Resources*. Boston, MA: Boston University School of Medicine.

(43) Kilpatrick, D. G., Ruggerio, k. J., Acierno, R., Saunders, B. E., Resnick, H. S., & Best, C.L. (2003). Violence and risk of PTSD, major depression, substance abuse/dependence, and comorbidity: results from the national survey of adolescents. *Journal of Consulting and Clinical Psychology*, 71, 692-700.

(44) Kohl, J. (1993). School-based child sexual abuse prevention programs. Journal of Family Violence, 8, 137-150.

(64) Putnam, F. (2003). Ten-year research updates review: Child sexual abuse. *Journal of the American Academy*

of Child and Adolescent Psychiatry, 42, 269-278.

(74) Simpson, C., Odor, r., & Masho, S. (2004 August*). Childhood Sexual Assault Victimization in Virginia.* Center for Injury and Violence Prevention. Virginia Department of Health.

Snyder, H. N. (2000). *Sexual assault of young children as reported to law enforcement*: Victim, incident, and offender characteristics. National Center for Juvenile Justice, U.S. Department of Justice.

(77) Sorensen, T. & Snow, B. (1991). How children tell: The process of disclosure in child sexual Abuse. Child Welfare League of America, 70, 3-15.

CPSIA information can be obtained at www.ICGtesting.com
Printed in the USA
LVOW10s0344150914

404058LV00001B/1/P